www.therkh.com

Available in paperback, e-book, and audiobook

About the Author

Raminder Kaur Hayre is a Surrey-born Canadian Punjabi who has made her global mark as a revolutionary trendsetter that, "plays by her own rules".

She is very passionate about her energetic business and prides herself on her well-rounded approach to dissecting the human condition.

Raminder embarked on her awakened path of being a spiritual healer for clients ranging in age from 20 to 70, from places near and far. She is also a lawyer, podcaster, and creator. Raminder built her brand on authenticity, empathy, and nuance.

She wrote this book to inform readers about how energy impacts daily practices and experiences.

Acknowledgements

I would like to thank everyone that has supported me in being the truest version of myself. There is blood family, and chosen family - I am lucky to have both.

Thank you to the teachers that pushed me, the mentors that supported my vision, and my friends and family for believing my purpose is worthy.

debunking the world we live in.

UNPACKING THE MATRIX AND SYSTEM.

By Raminder K. Hayre

The RKH

An original self-publication of RKH Consulting Services Ltd.

This book is based on personal experiences that resonate with the author and are not entirely based on fact or confirmed research. By reading this, any individual understands and assumes that the author is using her own narratives, examples, and modalities in what works for her. Any examples are general and do not expose privileged information of any sort - resonance is purely coincidental.

For any questions, please email: info@therkh.com or visit the contact form at: www.therkh.com

Chapters

debunking the world we live in.

UNPACKING THE MATRIX AND SYSTEM.

Cogito, ergo sum.

I think, therefore I am.

- René Descartes

Chapter 1

a journey to my ascension

October 18, 1991 - Surrey, BC, Canada

The crisp fall air loomed over the suburb, which would turn into a bustling city of samaritans worldwide. While there was certainty about new life being born into the Hayre family, the path I, the RKH, would follow was unknown.

Being raised in Surrey, BC, was an exciting experience. Sandwiched between an endless highway and New Westminster, the possibilities were either a skytrain or a car ride away. Many people stayed in these opportunities, but I eventually ventured off when the chance arose close to 18 years after I was born.

<u>Growing Up</u>

I always felt like I was out of place. There was this diplomatic and justice-seeking child who was often misunderstood. Attempts to be recognized seemed to fall on deaf ears of individuals who were either stuck in ego, perpetuated programmed beliefs, or understood the world differently than I did. The truth is that everyone sees the world through their unique lens based on their own experiences.

Even though my residence stayed the same, my school did not. I moved around among four different elementary schools in an attempt to find a place where my brother, cousin and I could shine. There were a few times I made this change individually, and it made me feel isolated. Looking back, it has led to maintaining a solid connection and network. People who are helping me fulfill my purpose now.

<u>Bullying</u>

I was bullied a lot throughout life. I was popular among friend groups but never in the family. The neglect turned into toxic relationships with abusive men. Looking back now, there was an understanding of gaining resilience through this adversity. A low sense of belonging within the home and with my cousins allowed me to explore these traumas as an adult.

DEBUNKING THE WORLD WE LIVE IN: UNPACKING THE MATRIX AND SYSTEM

Let's explore my career path now.

It is natural and almost guaranteed that bullying will be internalized.

From such a young age, we are programmed that being denied the chance to be authentic automatically leads to being questioned—and we are ridiculed for choosing ourselves. As we get older, my experience(s) shed light on how everyone's actions reflect and depict their own hardships, insecurities, or desire to fit into a predictable crowd.

We were raised on the principle of competition. It is our duty to deprogram that. This manuscript will explore this further.

-

The "black sheep" are always the most awakened ones - the reason being that they will not take crap from those around them. I always looked at it as a negative until my awakening. This shift in perspective occurred when I realized that I was troubled because people didn't want to hear the truth. It wasn't always because of me and my actions.

Granted, "black sheep" do not always make the best decisions.

Just think about the moments when you were ridiculed for:

- Speaking up for yourself;
- Setting boundaries;
- Asserting value;
- Saying no;
- Walking away etc...

The above are not negative things - they are ways we protect ourselves. It sounds messed up, but protecting ourselves means that we will trigger those who a) have a hard time advocating for themselves for any reason from fear, trauma, or uncertainty/discomfort, and b) do not want us to stop reassuring or validating them.

I have felt this so much in my life, and it was hard to get out of. Eventually, I just kept going and saw how much happier I was. As I got older, I became more fearful... I felt there was something to lose. I then awakened to the needed boundaries and spent a few years being strict about them.

DEBUNKING THE WORLD WE LIVE IN: UNPACKING THE MATRIX AND SYSTEM

People did not like this! It was also hard to hear people I was close to struggling with, realizing that they, too, had their own choices to make in life.

Whether it was not relying on me to do some of their inner work for them, reverse parenting, or keeping things "status quo" because it felt safer... I couldn't do it anymore.

I know that older generations find it difficult to have these boundaries in their lives. Additionally, many claim that the "pivotal generation", as I call it, is *disrespectful* in enforcing these changes.

The "pivotal generation" is the one doing the work to break the cycles and intergenerational patterns, which will be discussed later.

Those who put themselves in the spotlight to demand change will be revered but feared simultaneously. You always need to find out which direction those with boundaries will choose because it'll be about themselves!

-

DEBUNKING THE WORLD WE LIVE IN: UNPACKING THE MATRIX AND SYSTEM

How did I get to where I am?

This is a loaded question. Those who know me know it was hard for me to decide to become a lawyer and then switch to incorporating being a psychic healer. I mean... anyone could see that from a bird's-eye view.

Oh... if you don't know, now you do! Let's unpack this a bit.

-

My goal to be a lawyer started at the age of 12. Before that, I dabbled in wanting to be a dental hygienist (because I loved choosing colours for my braces, LOL!), an interior designer, or a chef, and then finally realized that a lawyer had to be it when I was chosen to "play a judge" in my high school law class.

I took it upon myself to start researching my path to getting there from age 14 onwards. I started to scout Canadian law schools and had my heart set on McGill or UBC. I wanted to do a dual J.D. (law graduate degree) and an MBA. I graduated high school and went to UBC at the Kelowna campus, where I did a Bachelor of Arts in Sociology.

DEBUNKING THE WORLD WE LIVE IN: UNPACKING THE MATRIX AND SYSTEM

My goal and intent were to move away as I was independent of how I grew up, and I wanted to fend for myself. I guess that is good and bad.

This choice was needed overall. I was 17, turning 18, and striving to gain a sense of who I was outside of circumstances that, quite honestly - left me very traumatized.

University was so hard after high school. I was almost always a straight-A student on the honour roll and the person that people cheated from in class. I thought that university would be the same.

It was not. Jumping from classrooms to a fly on the wall in lecture halls was not the daunting part - but the uncertainty was. I started to struggle with mental health and, at times, was medicated (and self-medicating). This was when I realized that the anxiety I felt growing up was indeed a "disorder." I quickly stopped medicine (not saying that you should) and tried my best to cope without it.

I worked hard and came to the UBC Vancouver campus after about 1.5 years of feeling stifled in growth around Kelowna. I graduated a semester early, which left me questioning when and where I would go to law school or for my MBA, as I was "early" for admissions in Canada.

I then found out about an Australian school named Bond that had a Canadian program. So, a mere three weeks after I graduated from UBC, I went to Bond to complete my Master's and then, subsequently, to law school. I probably shaved 1.5 years of schooling (at least)–and I didn't have to wait for the process here.

Living across the world started to teach me even more about myself. It also highlighted my mental health concerns. I was still the person that many relied heavily on, but I found it hard to rely on myself.

Upon returning to B.C. in 2016 after graduation, I worked a full-time job trying to find articling after I completed my NCA (equivalency) exams. It took me 1.5 years to find a job that paid me $1,000 monthly to article (the "apprenticeship" to become a lawyer). That should be illegal. But I took it since some friends have articled at firms for FREE!

After completing my articles, I struggled to complete PLTC. I was going through my awakening and a divorce, and I failed half of my bar program (PLTC). I had to redo it and make it through. After about five months, I miraculously landed a litigation associate job at a top-three downtown firm. How? My charisma, I guess. I manifested it.

The awakening moment was when I started watching YouTube videos about "What is my intuition?"

A vivid flashback of sitting on the couch reading The Goblet of Fire was striking in my mind... reminiscent of the times when parseltongue reminded me of my abilities.

I started to realize and play rewind on my life and how it brought me to where I was. This all started because of a romantic interest, and soon spiralled into me learning that I have psychic abilities unlocked. I was dumbfounded when I accepted that I had been gaslit or doubtful about my intuition.

Things I was told "I was wrong about" started manifesting in front of me. That was when I really knew.

Later that year, I met my twin-flame. At the moment of that meeting, I knew it was something different. It felt too familiar. I then learned that I had had my catalyst, which

was going to lead me to find out more about my life
purpose.

This was all happening around and during my associate job
mentioned above. It was a full-time career learning about my
spiritual side. I'd be in the office doing one thing and coming
home crying, trying to address another.

I continued to seek mentorship and even went on a two-
week cross-Canada train and road trip on my own. This is
when I started to realize that I could not put mountains
between how I was feeling. I needed to explore this fully
and thoroughly.

When I got back, I worked on enhancing my spiritual gifts
and admitted to myself that I was indeed a psychic and that
"the voice in my head" had been my spirit guides all along.
Decades of ignoring my guides had come to an end.

The main difference was that what I was hearing was not
anxiety. It was with integrity and stuff that I would not tell
myself. It was the truth and a different tone.

I started my coaching business as a "moonlighting" project
while I was still working the billable and big firm life. I was

burnt out. I convinced myself for a long time that I could do both...

During the plandemic (which I call it), I focused intensely on my spiritual business. Two weeks before the plandemic occurred, I quit one job (not knowing the world was about to shut down) and was left without work for a few months because no one was hiring. It was such a quick turnaround.

Us healers knew that something was going to happen... it just wasn't clear what it was.

-

Eventually, I moved on to contract work and opened my firm after being fired from my last big firm job. It was evident that I was let go every time I asserted my value (this happened in both big firm environments). It was a relief to be fired from my last "big law" job, because my guides had shown me signs for months in various ways that I had to focus on myself and the RKH brand.

Shortly after, I admitted to myself that it wasn't beneficial for me to continue living a double life. I was hindering my spiritual growth.

The hardest part was giving up my dream of becoming a judge. I had to choose between having a public opinion and a written one. Judges are not allowed to have a public expression in society. Time will tell what will stick

It was the deciding factor for me. My opinion is who I am, and my social media is my connection to the work I do... I had to decide.

I didn't feel useless for how hard I worked... but I felt bad for the 24-year-old who busted her ass to get three degrees. I made the complete switch at age 30 (going on 31)... so it was a huge dream which shifted. Everything transitioned once I allowed it.

So here I am now...

Chapter 2

the system "debunked"

You've probably heard the term "the system" a lot. To break it down into basic terms, it is the programming and society that we are born into. What's interesting about humanity and the 3D world is that many of us inherit these beliefs but are born to understand them better and dismantle them.

The above, while enlightening, requires a significant pivotal shift in disassociating with the norm to expand knowledge. We live in a 3d world, but we are higher-dimensional beings. What does this mean:

In short:

> - We are physical conduits of Source energy. We create our reality based on our belief system.

DEBUNKING THE WORLD WE LIVE IN: UNPACKING THE MATRIX AND SYSTEM

- The 3d world is a reflection of our ability to reflect and change.

- 5D consciousness is about manifesting and objectively appreciating that our thoughts precede our actions.

- A 5d thought process is beyond our physical circumstances, but doing what we *need* to achieve it - will be a powerful shift.

We can make the liberating (but challenging) choice to adjust our lives to become more fulfilling when acknowledging that the system we are born into trains us to be reliant through programming.

One thing that is hard for programmed individuals to believe and accept is that all systems are interlinked. We are born to be a part of the matrix, which is the simulation that the system creates.

Think of the matrix as a web that umbrellas over Earth like a game of Pacman, and "the system" is the institution that you are moving through in the game. Once you stop playing, you will better see its power and control over you.

The commonly understood structures in the systemic matrix we are born into:

1) Healthcare
2) Schools
3) Government
4) Law

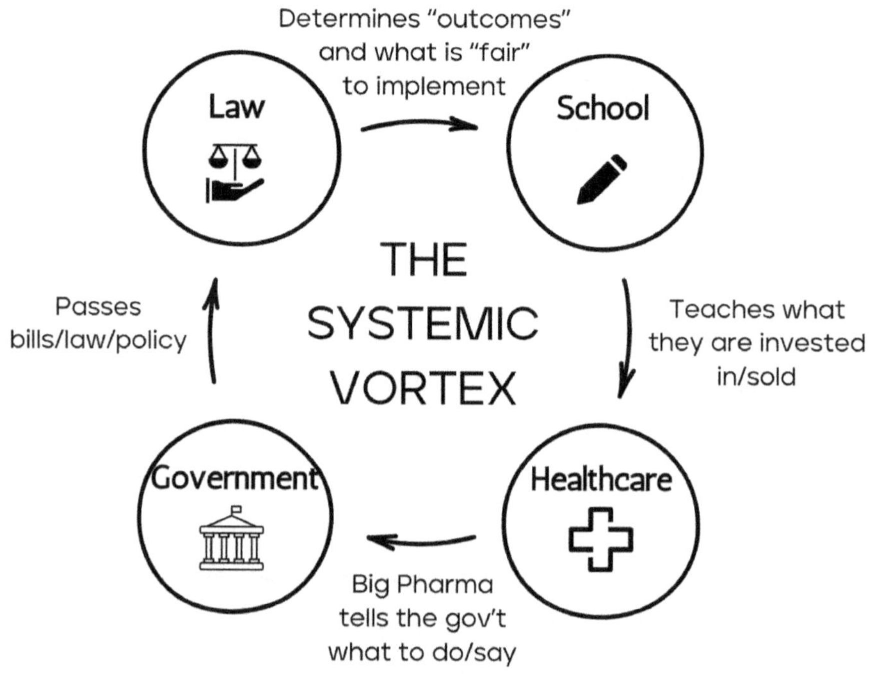

DEBUNKING THE WORLD WE LIVE IN: UNPACKING THE MATRIX AND SYSTEM

Observing this revolving door of a diagram will give you a perspective of the cyclical patterns. To understand how the system works, we must be able to view it from a birds-eye view. There is a requirement to step outside of this ferris wheel to disassociate from the assumption that these entities or institutions will provide you the privilege of being heard, and understood. The system was built with one priority: to create efficiency and to pump out people who will either succumb to pressures of mediocrity, push their limit(s) to make change, and/or put faith in the "golden handcuffs" to do the right thing. Golden Handcuffs: a seemingly reliable 9-5 job with low respect, benefits, and a bureaucratic hierarchy. Keep in mind that the system was purely colonial and male-focused. Even though times are different, this structure remains the same with "diverse" people. There is incremental growth because the foundation is unchanged.

It is hard to dissect and seek accountability, given that we are born to accept and participate in these systems. We are born to trust and want to do that. Why is that?

Because the system takes good, honest, and hard-working people and often strains them of their decision-making power. In turn, this leads to individual resentment, which can result in projecting insecurities and frustrations onto other people.

It is natural to believe in and look at the system as a reliable "big brother," for example. The truth is that they are playing that role literally—by controlling and watching our every move. This is partially why the pandemic (or, like I say, "plandemic") was such a turning point for accountability from a large population. Many people have been saying what has become known to others.

What impacts other places in the world will eventually affect us.

–

The Connection

The diagram above puts things into perspective. Still, it's crucial for us to understand the in-depth conditioning that occurs between the institutions that make up the system and matrix we live under.

Life is a video game. We only have to participate if we choose to be vulnerable characters who require a shadow of another to lead us. Much of the time, humans are taught that they don't know anything. This leads them far from their intuition, and then they base their existence on the institutions that tell them what they should believe.

Remember: Everything was once hypothetical and came to fruition because of one and then many belief systems. We have the ability to create that truth, but it will be ridiculed at the beginning of doing so.

-

Colonialism

People don't like to talk about race or supremacy as the root of a lot of things - but it is. While privilege comes in various forms, the greed of white supremacy has shaped how each and every one of us (no matter our skin colour) is told to behave. It just so happens that an injection of colour into the system did not and cannot resolve the perpetual issues.

For example, the RCMP was made to discipline the Indigenous, and so were the court systems. You cannot just add in a person who is brown, for example, and expect things to change if the structure of these institutions is faulty.

The way that decisions are made is intertwined like a spider web of supremacy energy. When challenged, there is pushback because of how the system will react to accountability. This is purely based on ego.

This will be covered further in Chapter 4, when we discuss intergenerational patterns.

-

Healthcare:

There is a reason that the system and many medical professionals look down on holistic health. Think about Paganism and "witchcraft" and how people who use holistic methods and spirituality are shut down from the mainstream.

It simply comes down to the fact that the medical system is rigged to make you believe and expose you only to what it feels is valuable. And what is valuable to the system? What brings money in?

In the U.S.A. and Canada (or any Commonwealth country), the importance of medical intervention and coercion is positioned to be the most valuable way to sustain life. For example, if you don't do this, this will happen. It is something that is ingrained into you.

Examples:

- If you don't vaccinate your child, you're a terrible parent.
- If you don't get the COVID-19 vaccine, you're okay with killing others.
- If you want to heal energetically, you don't care about your health.
- If you question the medical system, you are a conspiracy theorist.
- If you do your own research of the origins or intervention, you're wrong.

The above are all examples of programming and the "guilt trip," which automatically leads people to trust that their own judgement or compass is wrong. The goal of the system is to teach you that you cannot make your "own call" without confirmation of it from them, to validate and reassure you that that is right.

People who find holistic remedies or alternative options are not appreciated unless they are someone the system positions as "worthy" of making that decision. Look at the number of doctors who were disciplined or removed from the medical roll because they knew something deeper was going on.

Some of you are likely aware that corporations fund medical schools. They are also partially regulated through what the F.D.A. that these corporations see as acceptable. If you disagree with what they want to push, you risk your funding and the program's sustainability. Their beliefs are pushed through what you read. The ignorance bleeds on every page that promotes taking a pill over mitigating your stress levels. It is "your bad" if you question how your mindset and spirituality can better shape your livelihood - all because the system already has a solution for you - one that makes them money (eg: medicine, rules, etc...).

DEBUNKING THE WORLD WE LIVE IN: UNPACKING THE MATRIX AND SYSTEM

Schools:

We often need to appreciate or understand that each philosophical or sociological interpretation or theory was once a simple thought in the minds of theorists. It was only through implementation and global understanding that these principles became more of a fact.

School is also a set of goals that are programmed into the education system. This is why so many people home-school their children and guess what? They are ridiculed for doing so.

It was not until 2015 that Canada started to teach about Indigenous genocide as a requirement (at least in B.C.). History books had been filled with the triumph of the British, accolades for Christopher Columbus, and no mention of how the Church and supremacy have resulted in the deterioration of lineage for people of colour.

When mentioned in the present day, it is ignored. A lot of unconscious bias occurs because of what one is willing to accept about the place(s) one lives.

DEBUNKING THE WORLD WE LIVE IN: UNPACKING THE MATRIX AND SYSTEM

<u>Think about this loop:</u>

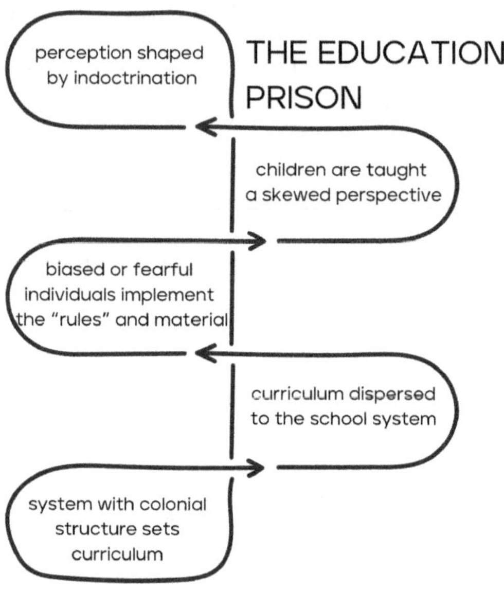

The above can also happen in any further schooling, depending on your studies. A deep program could occur if there is a limited buffer between allowing for an expansion or diversion in one's thought process and forcing people to stay "status quo." The system is triggered by people with a unique thought process simply because it cannot empathize and was built on the protocol that there is only one line of thought.

DEBUNKING THE WORLD WE LIVE IN: UNPACKING THE MATRIX AND SYSTEM

Government:

Government, law, and policy are three words that are often heard together. There is an assumption that they are a unit but an expectation of exclusivity. This "division of powers" is something that we assume will address areas of conflict, but it has started to become more convoluted than seen by the naked eye before.

People worldwide tend to trust the government to ensure that equitable measures are taken for the safety, well-being, and understanding of citizens. The irony is that while there is a belief in "division," the truth of corporate interest comes into play when the law is not adequately considered in policy decisions.

So, what is "policy"? It is legislation, rules, outlines, or guides that are formed by the government either through public interest or politicians, which we assume will consider the law. While it is common sense to presume this, it is essential to know that policies and legislation have been found to be unethical or a breach on many occasions.

This is where we can see how inequitable solutions, racism, and privilege are intertwined within citizens' daily expectations. There is an inbred trust, but it really should not be. A layperson knows a lot better than many of the people introducing these "mandates," so to speak, for specific demographics.

The Division and Separation of Powers

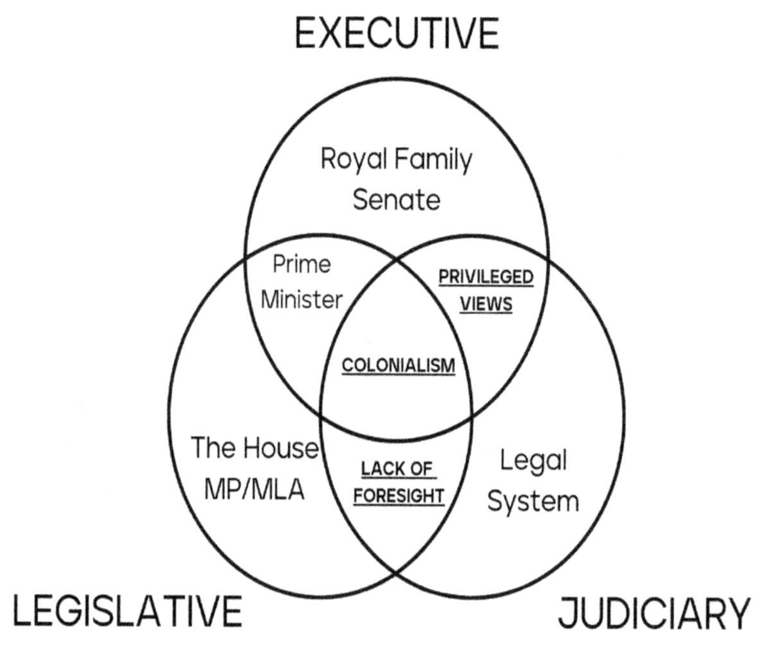

DEBUNKING THE WORLD WE LIVE IN: UNPACKING THE MATRIX AND SYSTEM

The division (or distribution/separation) of powers are the heads of institutions that create our system. They are meant to be separate for neutrality but are often intertwined. They comprise a "board of national governance," which can be broken down into provincial/territorial and federal matters. For example, individual insurance plans are provincial, but healthcare as a whole is a federal "right." The provincial government can make rules, but the provincial and federal legal systems can trump and strike down anything against your fundamental rights. NB: different countries have different structures, but most Commonwealth and "Western" nations lend a similar structure. This is to build on a base-level understanding of the ranks. The <u>OVERLAPS</u> in the diagram in capitals are additions based on opinion and are not taught as fact within the system.*

Many ask, "Why would this be passed if it's illegal?" It isn't that there is a callous attempt to skirt the law - but it is not entirely a prerequisite for politicians to ensure that the Charter is thoroughly considered. Additionally, thinking members of the public is something that is supposed to be done but often needs to be done. Protests, campaigns, and calls to action occur after citizens and advocates realize there is something to delve deeper into - the power is always in our hands, not theirs.

DEBUNKING THE WORLD WE LIVE IN: UNPACKING THE MATRIX AND SYSTEM

Your position is threatened by the system and its tolerance of your adversity. The same occurs in each of the system's structures: healthcare, school, government, and law.

Remember the bullying discussed in Chapter 1? The systems use this mentality and indoctrination to get an advantage over you. If you were not validated or assured, or if you haven't worked through your trauma, then you will grow up *seeking* authority figures who will console you into trusting yourself. This *doesn't* happen - it just gets worse.

Have you ever had a boss that you wanted to love you and show you compassion? It is because you are trying to comfort the inner child who didn't receive that support growing up. An unhealed part of you is seeking to be uncovered and assured.

Have you sought the system to validate your feelings and worth? This tends to be the "little you" seeking community acceptance.

The disappointment you feel when Trudeau or Biden oversteps is wishing that someone would do the right thing.

A real test is eliminating their power and trusting your own sovereignty to make the decisions that are best for you.

But how do you do that? By healing. It is less about ignoring "them", and more about finding yourself. Your voice is just as important.

Healing is a multifaceted and lifelong vocation. There is no one-step rule for healing the parts of yourself that seek community acceptance. It is buried within generations and lineage, only to come up at times of adversity. We are given chances to dismantle our programming in those opportunities that lead us to anger, fear, and resentment.

Getting through those "negative emotions" will require the perseverance your grandmother wishes she had. It will involve facing the resistance that millions of people before you were unable to challenge due to the system and patriarchy. Keep in mind that all of that power your ancestors had is something that you currently hold.

Chapter 3

what is the matrix + divine orchestration?

Many of you may think of the Matrix movie when you ask "What the matrix is." If it helps, think of the film as a guide for how we are programmed and how our Universe is essentially a database of our projection.

Whether we believe in God, Source, the placebo effect, the law of attraction, etc....., it is essential to know that the dominant and baseline energy for these beliefs and/or prayers is an understanding that we can create our reality based on our faith in something.

DEBUNKING THE WORLD WE LIVE IN: UNPACKING THE MATRIX AND SYSTEM

We can consider the system and matrix interchangeable in the sense that they are all about a level of control. However, the matrix is more of an overarching umbrella, whereas the system is the players that enforce the matrix.

What we resonate with will guide our direction within the simulation. There is no right or wrong. Even extremists have a great deal of purpose, which brings clarity to those around them (usually in the opposite direction if they interact outside their echo chamber).

NB: An echo chamber will limit your growth and perspective if you constantly seek validation from others' belief systems without empathizing that each person has their own experience and Truth. This is a way that people remain unchallenged because they only want to interact with those who do not have them question their perspective. Of course, this is all within reason and is outside blatant discrimination, racism, and the like.

Think of life as a video game with the below diagram:

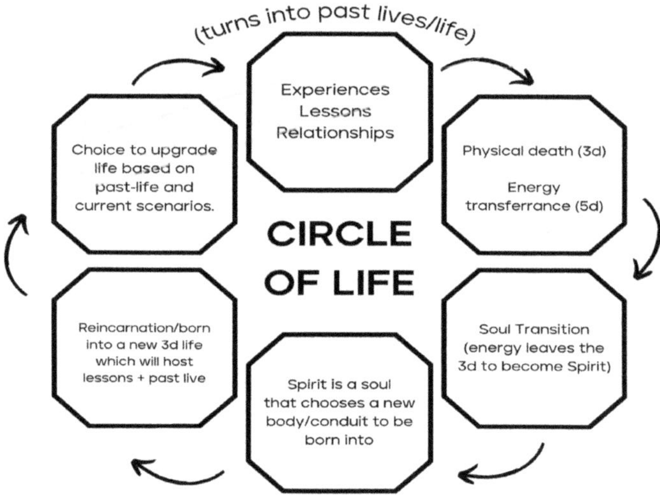

The above diagram shows you how energy works. It is a revolving door of reincarnation and energetic exchanges with old and new people that are a part of your purpose. You'll have many interactions that involve jiving with people you know from past life experiences. Your life depends on reliving, redefining, and growing from those interactions/relationships.

The main thing to consider is that there is life after death. Have you ever had those "deja vu" moments? Those are your conscious remembrances from past lives or situations that you have been in before. That "ah ha" or "wtf" is teaching you that you are manifesting your reality - this is often in dreams too.

Have you seen something in a dream that comes to life? Your consciousness is the most online when you are sleeping, and it is when your guides give you downloads and messages about where your life can/will be. Your guides will also show you symbolism to take a better direction in your life.

This resonance also occurs when you pick up a new hobby, job, or craft that you are automatically good at but have not done in this lifetime before. It is often a remembrance from a past life coming to fruition in your new reality. Your soul's energy remembers your skill level, as you have already learned it in another life.

Think of your life like a grid (below)—these are timelines that are possible for you. Any direction, in any way, can lead you on a different trajectory.

THE GRID

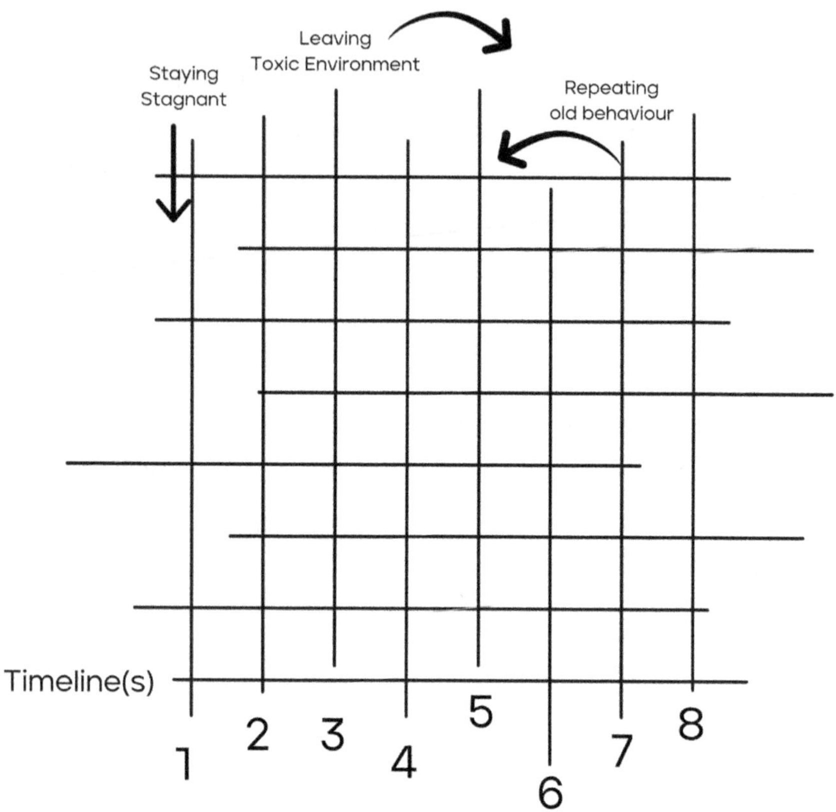

We like to believe in fate but forget that we create it by making aligned decisions. There is beauty in making choices that allow us to manifest something we have been dreaming of. This could be choosing, leaving, altering, or moving from people/places/things. There are unlimited realities based on a single life choice we make. If you choose to work at

McDonald's, you'll have a different life experience and meet alternative opportunities than if you had a job at a doctor's office.

It may help to think of each timeline as a different level in a video game. Each has its quirks, perspectives, and advantages/disadvantages.

-

You are your divine creator. When you hear "co-creation," you may ask yourself, "What does that even mean?". It is an allowance of opportunities the divine brings to you based on your level. If you continue to "play small" or swim in the same energy which is holding you back, there is no way that they can bring you to a different destination (at least not without force). For example, A parent may tell you to get out of the pool, and if you don't listen, they'll eventually grab you and force you to dry off.

The Universe will do the same if you stay somewhere too long—like when you get fired, cheated on, lied to, deceived, or more. It isn't that life hates you; you were avoiding the bright detour or alternate route signs along the way.

DEBUNKING THE WORLD WE LIVE IN: UNPACKING THE
MATRIX AND SYSTEM

Without a doubt, there are many times when you look in hindsight and say, "Wow, I am so glad that happened," or, "Why did I stay there for so long?" - those are the moments of clarity in which you have the chance to appreciate the blatant redirection that the divine forced on you. If you are consistently manifesting and wishing for a better life, it is best to believe that whatever is not meant for you will eventually clear and/or make your life miserable in the hopes that you will leave it.

Not to contradict the above, but there are always opportunities for a relationship to transform if both parties choose to step into a new timeline. The choice is yours to shift onto yours—the rest will follow that new trajectory on the grid.

Relationships require two people - and free will plays a huge factor in one's ability to co-create with you. Those decisions are always a part of a bigger purpose and journey.

Can we get into a journey that isn't meant for us? Not entirely. This goes for any style of relationship.

It is all about the perspective on why we are at or where we are. Since we co-create, our path is determined by our action(s). Sometimes, we have a detour, roadblock, or acceleration on the drive - depending on the forecast and how other factors on the road interact with the energy. If your new vibration (projection, expression, and esteem) toward the Universe knocks something out of the way, trust that it is meant to be.

Purpose is a way we act, it is not a destination. This purpose includes the people we meet, the relationship(s) we hone, the jobs that come to us and so forth. Many individuals base their whole lives on "becoming" something when the one necessary thing is our commitment to evolve. If we stop this process, we hinder our blessings. While people commend themselves and others for staying in one spot for too long, it is rarely acknowledged that doing so can limit what they seek—their destiny.

Each of us is built with a specific purpose in our human design. The Universe sort of "sparks" our genetic makeup with a bolt of energetic programming that we are meant to discover in each life. Our ability to figure this out is tied to our willingness to do things beyond the norm. Unsurprisingly, the system and matrix were curated by low-vibrational energy—that development was meant to keep people stuck

and out of purpose (the golden handcuffs spoken about
earlier).

Being able to acquiesce or progress will allow anyone the
chance to form an umbrella of positive energy around them.
This envelope of light and positive vibes will allow anybody
an opening to build a life and vocation around this purpose.
The actual test is whether an individual will go through the
difficult path of eliminating the people, places, and
things ("the trilogy" from hereon, in - write this down so you
don't forget later!) to get to that point. It is nearly impossible
to accept your purpose and path without going through the
turbulence of drastic life changes which allow you to get
there.

These changes often include leaving a secure/stable job, a
toxic relationship, working on value or self-esteem, or
choosing aligned decisions daily, even if that means puddling
through addiction, trauma, creating boundaries, and more.

The matrix will do almost anything to keep you from living a
high-vibe life because knowing that you can co-create means
you will use discernment in the rules and regulations you
wish to enforce in your life (systemic control, as discussed
earlier).

DEBUNKING THE WORLD WE LIVE IN: UNPACKING THE MATRIX AND SYSTEM

Let's dive a little into vibration.

Vibration is what helps us attract what we want.

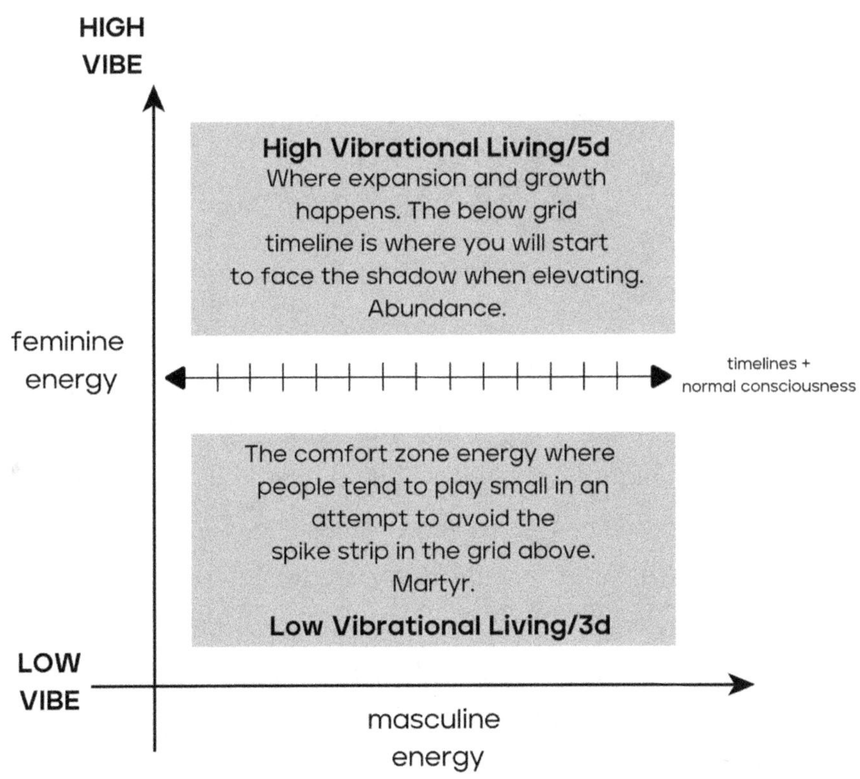

DEBUNKING THE WORLD WE LIVE IN: UNPACKING THE MATRIX AND SYSTEM

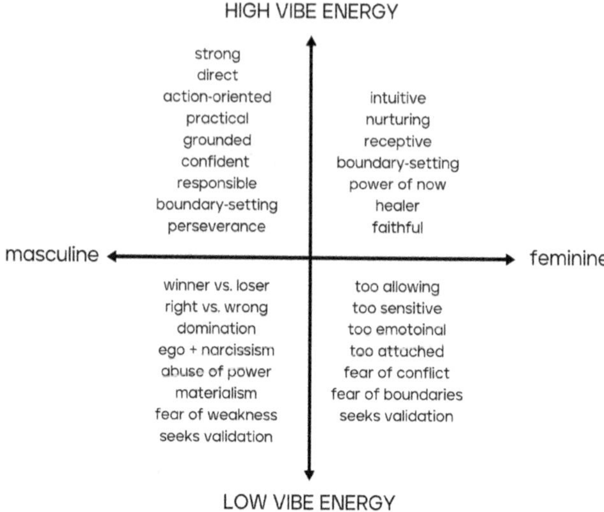

You will be met with a lot of resistance in the way of aligning with a higher vibration. This is because any shadow energy will test you. I like to refer to this as "dementor energy" (if you're familiar with Harry Potter). There is a persistence that high vibrational truth seekers need to exude to eliminate the dark (or parts of it) throughout life. The shadow cannot be avoided - it can only be reduced or shifted. Spiritual bypassing means living life skirting the hardship, thinking it is "high-vibe" or "in alignment." Continuing to defer the confrontation of something holding you back will cause it to pile up. Consider late fees and interest - this is what it does to your life.

There is a distinguishable difference between creating/maintaining boundaries and avoiding conflict. Confrontation is a natural and necessary part of understanding the role of the divine and the matrix in our lives. The matrix includes patriarchy and colonialism. For example, choose to isolate yourself from any interference completely. You will avoid living a life of fulfillment because you won't give yourself and your inner child permission to heal parts of yourself that you have been programmed with.

A huge part of who you are meant to become is on the other side of this healing. For example, your romantic relationship(s) will trigger you in ways that will open you up about the traumas meant to be healed. You need to discern what is abusive or toxic.

NB: Toxic and abusive relationships are, unfortunately, a part of getting to know yourself better. If you are in an incarnation that holds past-life energy which is rooted in supremacy, patriarchy, imbalance, etc... you will have to dismantle that programming or expectation in present life. Growing up in a healthy or more conscious home is a gift from the Universe for graduating to levels in the matrix after learning lessons. Ex: If your parents did the work to grow into a respectful and conscious dynamic, you will have the privilege and/or experience of passing that vivacious energy on in the next generation. *This does not mean you should allow toxicity.*

-

Many want to buy their way into abundance, success, or accolades. In reality, most of this can authentically come when one chooses to live a life of alignment. It is a misconception that hard work is not required. Once you achieve a standard vibration, you are able to manipulate the simulation to provide you with what you seek positively.

Rather than doing the work to unpack this possibility, people will buy what they need for external gratification. This could include cars, a big house, fancy possessions, awards (yes, you can buy awards), and even people.

The matrix programs you to believe that you need these things and essentially grooms many "celebrities" to show you the attainable calibre of life. They don't glorify the amount of hard work that can go into receiving or achieving a type of status. This does not mean that nepotism or privilege does not exist; it minimizes the stress of attaining one's highest potential. People who have made vulnerable documentaries about their addiction and/or mental health battles are often criticized for opening up; hence, being judged. One reason for this is that the system and these "groomers" are fearful of this information being accessible to everyone - addiction is a by-product of corruption and toxicity.

So, what is "programming"?

It is an ingraining of your personality and how you view the world. From the moment you are born, you are (if your parents are not awake) likely taught that your power to succeed and be healthy is beyond your control. If it is in your control, it is only through hard work, etc... This is false programming. Since we are born with our success and purpose, that means we don't need the system to validate that - we spend a lot of time hoping they will guide us there. We are our guidance system!

As a baby, you are vulnerable and given vaccines. You and your parents are programmed to believe that better health is acquired through intervention. This doesn't mean modern medicine doesn't work, but it is outdated and keeps you fighting against energies that don't exist anymore. → Then you go to school, which teaches you what the government says is vital to know → Gender roles are often affirmed in patriarchal homes → Questions about "who you want to be" are enforced → Your life is built upon you becoming a "powerful person" which often involves more schooling which entails a lot of skewed information.

From experience, questioning theories and having an individual perception have been criticized. How can it be that an application of something subjective has a right or wrong answer? One is then graded on whether they view the world the same as the elite/those who have bought into the system to push an agenda.

This is programming.
Well, how could the divine take part in programming? Can't they get rid of it?

Not entirely.

The purpose of programming is to teach individuals how to overcome it. It sounds stupid because it is. Look at it as a "right of passage." When you're born into the simulation, and your soul chooses to be, your lessons and purpose are built into the trilogy. Once you have learned most of the lessons, 3d Earth becomes pointless, you graduate and become Source Energy in the Universe and start to guide people.

You must complete your lessons and become purely energy. Again, the Universe and Earth is a giant video game. If you are unwilling to do the work to better understand how you came to be and why your life is the way it is, you wouldn't have been born here at all.

Even though there is hardship, there is also a lot of abundance and fulfillment. We must reframe our minds to participate in life with the intention of being happy. Think about whether your programming has ever led you to contentment. Probably not.

That's enough to understand the deep requirement for healing. It is what allows us to choose sovereignty and individualism in the pursuit of meaningful and soul-aligned connection.

Life is essentially a resurrection. There is no true answer about how we "came to be" in the first place. We were once energy that metamorphosed into a physical being based on where our polarities were. The polarities are the masculine and feminine energies in the chart above.

There is a lot of emphasis on gender in the 3d world - let's be clear that gender doesn't exist in energy. Many people get hooked into "male" and "female" biology, and while it is true, energetically, we are fluid. This plays a role in how different people show up in their identity. It is not to condone dangerous programming but to allow people to be seen and heard based on their feelings. Those who are innocently living life are doing so in alignment, and the friction they meet with homophobic individuals is a part of their purpose to dismantle. Imagine being a person of high vibration and people trying to pigeonhole you. It is exhausting. *˄This is a generalization.*

As implied above, the polarities are regardless of gender. We all have masculine and feminine traits that make us who we are. They are categories that we try to balance throughout life. The matrix will try to pull us in one or the other direction - the goal is to balance life in a way that feels content. It may not be 50/50 all the time, but it is important to act when needed, and receive when required.

DEBUNKING THE WORLD WE LIVE IN: UNPACKING THE MATRIX AND SYSTEM

When we are born into the 3D, we are magnetized to the lessons that will teach us the most. The lessons that are necessary will come to us, and it is our duty to grasp the polarities in the energy and alchemize it into something meaningful, purposeful, and transformative.

Being "too alpha" in anything will create glitches in the matrix. It will short-circuit your system and programming to open you up to be more in your feminine energy. "Alpha" is a robust masculine trait, and people are successful in 3d life when they focus on being "the top dog." The system was curated for people to live in their masculine energy, which hinders their ability to be in their feminine energy or receptive mode to attract easily.

Why would the system or matrix want you to have ease when it has taught you to be submissive and reliant? Debunking the myths of success will eventually manifest in your life as an abundance you do not have to fight for or work countless hours to achieve.

Chapter 4

intergenerational patterns +

colonialism

Did you know that a lot of the trauma that you endure is connected to generations before you? Well, if you didn't, now you do.

Energy is so powerful that the transfer between each generation can trigger you into a specific level or category of healing. If the generation before you did the work to heal (which they do, even if 1%), you will face a more "diluted" version of the trauma. It doesn't mean it'll be easy, but it'll be adjusted with a thread of the same energy. This 1% of healing can be like setting boundaries, leaving a situation, breaking patterns or structure, and more.

We may question why things were not entirely different and why they have to impact us, but we must remember how hard it is to make significant changes that align with our values and the resources needed to do so. This is why the patriarchy has so much control over us; it's also the reason colonialism still succeeds.

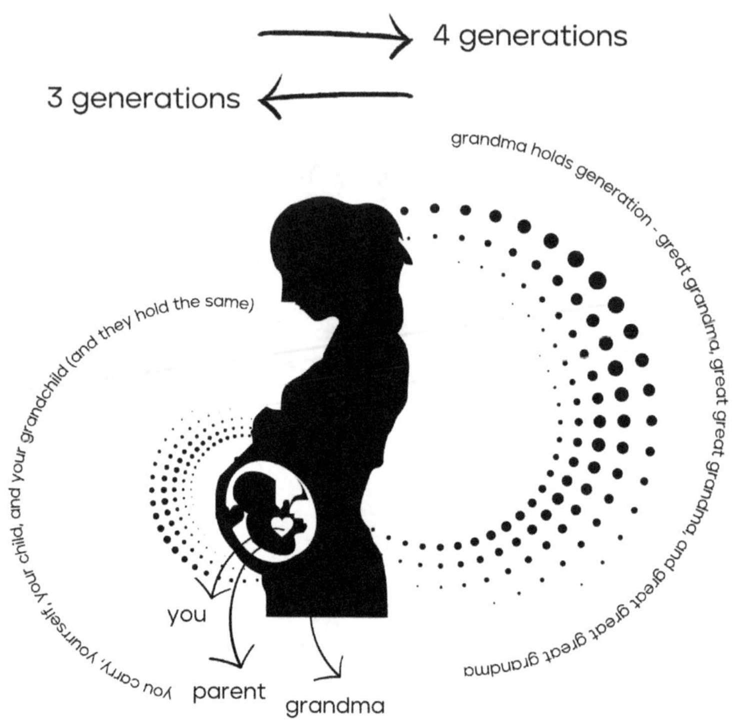

Even though the above graph is a woman, take note that men also carry the same energy too. It isn't one-sided, but the visual of a woman's body is helpful. A grandma can also carry a male who would be impacted by energy - the trauma imposed by a male or female onto your grandma is something that is in your DNA as well. Any impactful energy is not limited to being in the womb space but is also transferred through physical touch, emotion, verbal communication, etc... P.S. it doesn't matter whether a fetus can procreate - the fact that they are developing is enough to host the energy of the next generation. The 3D world is not the Universe!

Women were programmed to be submissive, and it became even worse for those who essentially weren't British to fit into colonialism effortlessly. Why? Because the intersection of factors made the situation a lot worse. Being a white female in Britain during colonial times was vastly different than being a brown woman from the slums of India under British rule.

Consider the below to assess your privilege:

FACTORS IN OPPRESSION

Are you a woman?	yes	no
Are you a person of colour?	yes	no
Did you grow up in scarcity?	yes	no
Are you an immigrant?	yes	no
Are you a first-generation?	yes	no
Did you have to work hard for your first job?	yes	no
Were you raised in an impoverished area?	yes	no
Were your parents emotionally unavailable?	yes	no
Were your parents physically absent?	yes	no
Did you often starve/feel hungry?	yes	no
Have you been emotionally abused?	yes	no
Have you been physically abused?	yes	no
Have you been mentally abused?	yes	no
Have you been verbally abused?	yes	no
Are you often gaslit or manipulated?	yes	no
Have you been cheated on?	yes	no
Did you witness abuse in your home?	yes	no
Do you have phobias or fears?	yes	no
Were you bullied growing up?	yes	no
Is english your second language?	yes	no
Do you have an accent that is made fun of?	yes	no
Do you have a hard time with technology?	yes	no
Is it hard for you to get answers to questions?	yes	no
Are resources readily available for you?	yes	no
Do you have a good support system?	yes	no
Would your family/friend answer similar to you?	yes	no

If you wish to grab a pen or pencil, you can circle or mark the intersectional factors that apply to you or others around you. Reflect on how life could be vastly different. The goal is not to justify anything but to understand the unconscious biases that play a massive role in how society functions. It is often the person that is "more oppressed" that does the educating for the "more privileged" to understand their viewpoint. This would be the case in any scenario, and we could switch based on it, too. Notice how many "yeses" vs. "nos." The more "yeses," the higher the chance(s) of being oppressed in various ways. P.S. This list is not exhaustive or to pigeonhole - please treat it like an objective exercise if you're triggered as to why and how it hits your self-esteem or value of self.

-

Many people live in their own bubble, and ego can hold them back from looking at those around them with compassion. It takes a lot of strength and empathy to take a step back and surround your senses with the possibility that life experiences, emotions, and trauma are different for each and every person in this world. Some people have it "worse" and others "better." It is interesting to know that the levels of ease are often based on how many times you have been on Earth. If you focus only on the 3d world and are financially abundant but have no emotion or empathy (like many billionaires), you are not on a healing journey. When people come back and reincarnate to have some struggle, this is mainly because they are meant to go through the resistance of becoming a spiritual being; hence, they lose a lot to gain a lot. This is a paradox and only makes sense once you are at that threshold. Healers also go through intense deprogramming.

Think of it as a recovery. You keep returning to Earth to disassociate from materialism and lead your life by emotion. Many people do the opposite. You can gain a lot of success, but the cost is often being stuck in the system, under the rule of a man in this colonial structure we have become used to - at least in the West.

Who actually wants to work a 9-5 to seek permission from a department to take time off once or twice a year and make enough only to make ends meet? Basically, no one. It has just become the norm. The colonial structure ingrained this mentality into society because it wanted to produce workers. The people who want certain things to be taught within the system are the ones who create the programming because they have the resources to pay people to write books, give opportunities to those who agree with them, and provide them continued reassurance.

These "facts" are then sold to schools for a profit and taught to everybody. We must individually address and come to terms with this cycle –this is why value and resistance are not respected. They want things to remain "status quo."

That baseline is also what keeps intergenerational patterns and programming revolving. It requires a lot of strength and a "no effs given" attitude to persevere through obstacles that have been put in your way from before you were born.

Examples:

Grandfather was in a war and faced being killed every day (the nervous system is unregulated and faces a lot of anxiety) → Dad, growing up, faced that anxiety when grandfather was home and started to find ways to limit uncertainty (emotionally controlling, and narrow-minded) → Son faces a lot of limitation of freedom as he grows older (turns into a people-pleaser and doesn't want to tick people off).

You can see how the energies dilute/adjust through the generations, but they all have similar underlying notes of fear, anxiety, and not wanting to "rock the boat" in any way. These patterns can happen for as many as seven generations in either direction because three generations impacted your grandparents, and at least three generations after you will be impacted as well.

The great thing is that doing the work of healing will allow the next generations to make positive changes! Persevering through intergenerational obstacles gives the generations above you the chance to change, too. If there is a willingness, then you will see that they have become more aligned versions of themselves because your shift in energy helps project light onto them (something they probably have not seen much of).

While changes bring good, they also come with challenges. People are scared to look at how their actions, lives, and trauma have impacted them, and others are scared to accept that people around them have their own experiences with the same. The projection has become so normalized that it has led many to live in a false reality.

For instance, people have immigrated to the West from Asian countries but expect that the next generation(s) will continue to follow every expectation from their "motherland" without accounting for growing up in a completely new environment. This causes a lot of friction in patriarchal homes because a lot of Asian beliefs, for example, are rooted in men being superior. Women have a lot more flexibility (not that Asians do not have any in many places they are from), and it is normalized in the West. The patriarchy has kept many people rigid in their roles and expectations. Altering those to mirror a different upbringing can be met with hostility - that is why many families grow apart.

The beliefs that coincide with these expectations will be highlighted more as we go through the great planetary awakening. We are currently in a huge shift that will continue until 2030. The life we know is shifting forever, and we are being given all the tools to make more aligned decisions. Issues arise when we seek change but are unwilling to make sacrifices. If we know that something in the trilogy is holding us back, we must confront it to move forward.

People don't like confrontation - that is what leads us to face more trauma. There are opportunities to set boundaries and advocate for ourselves at every corner. This makes it challenging. The fear we feel when addressing our needs and boundaries is something that has been fought against for centuries. The rules put in place are things that the colonial or patriarchal structure implemented to give healers and powerful rulers limited access to changing their lives for the better.

Have you ever heard of witches, pagans, or spiritualists being sanctioned in past or current lives? It is because they have always known of the true power of the Universe. It is not something that is ruled by the system.

Why would the system want you to know you have the power to create within?

The system spends billions, if not trillions of dollars a year, collectively implementing blocks to keep you from accessing your inner power. Whether that is through the content you read, creating health fiascos like the plandemic, giving you a dopamine release you keep chasing, etc... The fixation on instant gratification keeps you ungrounded and away from your center.

It is on you to come back to your body. Rushing around, basing your emotions on a fast response, making sure everyone around you is taken care of, or avoiding uncertainty will keep you in a cyclical pattern until you choose to get off the ferris wheel and observe how your nervous system is impacted.

DEBUNKING THE WORLD WE LIVE IN: UNPACKING THE MATRIX AND SYSTEM

Generations before you could not regulate their nervous system because they were in constant "fight or flight" mode. Fleeing famine, war, genocide, apartheid, colonialism, and abuse led to people being in a holding pattern with shields up.

The privilege of assessing your circumstances while holding space for growth is the most powerful tool you have. That is how you get your autonomy in decision-making back. The matrix system and colonialism will create several roadblocks to keep you from getting there. It will tell you that you need medication, validation, the newest gadget, or an expensive promotion (which can lead to a mental health crisis) to achieve the ultimate level of success.

Fun fact. It never f*cking ends, dude.

One of the main reasons you are sitting here and reading this today is because you have the right, ability and patience. Trust that people unwilling to raise their consciousness or awareness would not sit through being told that their creation is based on their mindset or ability to see the world's programming.

DEBUNKING THE WORLD WE LIVE IN: UNPACKING THE MATRIX AND SYSTEM

Are you not taking it seriously? It doesn't matter. You are shifting your subconscious programming and bringing things to the forefront of your mind by reconsidering your genetic makeup, your mindset or system's control over you, and why you are in control of your destiny.

-

Life is not a crystal ball, but you can lead yourself through intuition.

Intuition is blocked when we age because conditioning and programming attempt (which is often successful) to keep us from our alignment.

If you're in alignment, then you are powerful - the system wants all of the power. Take yours back.

Think of the colonial structure's origin as an entity that was given all of the good cards during poker. They were able to leverage, steal, manipulate, and multiply all of their efforts to gain from their "opponents." This then put them at the top of the category, and no one was able to catch up because the cells of their success kept duplicating like a disease. Eventually, they were overpowering everybody.

DEBUNKING THE WORLD WE LIVE IN: UNPACKING THE MATRIX AND SYSTEM

Look at the plandemic as a manufactured scenario that the governments used to try and stifle people. They succeeded for the most part because it was foreign. The older generation(s) were used to it, and those who were speaking up and questioning were in the minority until more recently. Questions are met with "the hand" unless you validate the oppressor's motives.

The system also controls the media, becoming the "matrix of information." Think of the system as software that casts a net over the most susceptible people.

Colonialism also bought out the media. This isn't just white/British originators; it is any group that feels that they are better (e.g., Zionists in Israel, Hindutva extremists in India, any biased or politically led CBC promoters in Canada). Because they own the news, they own the outpour. Since people are raised to trust the news, the information is first seen as fact. It is then believed, questioned, glossed over, or turned off. It depends on each person's malleability, intuitive presence, and analytical thinking skills. As mentioned, those in an earlier incarnation of life are more likely to align with programming and blind faith because there are lessons to come within their purpose (in this or another lifetime).

Everyone has free will, but it depends on the lessons that your soul wants to live through, too.

-

Why would our soul want to live through these restrictions? Honestly, there is no answer. Your mind is as vast as the Universe. Permit yourself to soar, contemplate the beauties of life, and the possibility of why we are here now.

Philosophy promotes the belief that the ability to think about something is enough to know that it can exist.

This means that you are also able to manifest a life that is beyond what you currently see. The divine can assist with those things if you can look at life beyond the matrix (or even the grid in the previous chapter).

Your ability to create that life is determined by your perseverance in confronting the resistance that has been planted in you from previous generations. Feeling discomfort is not a sign of unalignment—it can be the invisible barrier you are breaking to achieve what you seek. On the contrary, you may be nudged to go a different way or detoured, and that is okay, too.

Remember that if you feel that a direction is the right way and you can feel why, then you will probably face the reaction your ancestors had to heal and clear it and create it. It doesn't mean it has to be the only way you manifest what you seek, but it will be a part of your purpose in getting there.

We put so much pressure on defining critical moments as a 3d society that we need to remember to embrace the ripples in time of the Universe that allow us to get to where we are.

For example, I had an elementary school friend reach out to me the other day and say this:

"I was thinking about the pull of energies and how sometimes you can pinpoint a moment where things shifted.

I had one of those a couple weeks ago while sitting in an energy healing with _____.

I realized I wouldn't have been in that room had I not met ___, and I wouldn't have met ___ had she not worked with you."

We wouldn't have met if my parents had not sent me to the school I attended only for grade 6.

This ripple took almost 13 years to manifest!

-

Many people do not like it when parents live vicariously through them—and for good reason. It usually errs on the side of becoming overbearing rather than speaking about how they want to provide a child with opportunity. We are getting there! Many of our ancestors had goals and dreams, but they were put on hold due to various factors.

Now, we live in an environment in many places of the world where individuals can dream of "making it big" to achieve their aspirations no matter their background. It was sometimes different. Perhaps it was a lack of guidance, the oppressive factors talked about earlier, and/or no assurance that they wouldn't end up dead.

DEBUNKING THE WORLD WE LIVE IN: UNPACKING THE MATRIX AND SYSTEM

Remember that "flight or fight" mode and anxiety are passed down through generations, and they will become activated. Our purpose can help us unleash the power to deal with it, and sometimes, it comes in different ways. There is no "cookie-cutter" formula or guarantee that we will persist through all obstacles or challenges in this lifetime—that's why we come back again!

You may be wondering whether your ancestors will come back to clear their trauma or anxieties, and the answer is YES. They are in the same time circle of life as you, which means that they loosen the reins in each life, and you will energetically benefit from those differences and shifts, too.

We are all doing work together and simultaneously. You have probably heard the terms, "You are the company you keep" or "You are a projection of the five people you surround yourself with. "These phrases indicate that your energetic capacity is mirrored in how you view those around you.

People who play small stay small—often because of those around them. If you converse with people who motivate you, you'll likely find inspiration to "be bigger" or "do more." This doesn't mean you are constantly pushing against your present moment; instead, you are allowing yourself to dream beyond what you see in your immediate circle.

There is dark and light everywhere that we go. We pick up on light codes when we travel or go for a local walk. People around us exude a different energy and can pass their lights onto us like a bubble attaching to the bubble next to it. It can inspire you - but if you are unaligned, dark energy can seep into you, too. That's why it is important to use discernment and surround yourself with healthy/positive energy to tell what will work for you.

Sometimes, what is good for you is stepping away from intergenerational patterns and hardship. You don't have to push against the grain all the time—you can decide to step out. The difference between clearing/healing and stepping out is in the moment when you decide that you deserve better. Sometimes, we do this earlier than possible, which is "spiritual bypassing."

What that term means is that people want to avoid doing the healing work or feeling any shadow part of themselves, so they do whatever it is to avoid. Avoidance is a deferral. It doesn't clear but builds. Stepping out is when you have continued to be in a situation, learned the lesson, and then created boundaries not to have it a part of your reality anymore.

Intergenerational programming is deeply rooted in people-pleasing, a lack of boundaries, putting themselves last, and avoiding making difficult decisions.

The decisions you make can be the turning point in breaking a generational curse that kept your ancestors or lineage stuck. You then get to do what is aligned for you and empower the generations before and after you to do the same. NB: People in the generations before you may become distanced, or you could have certain boundaries if they are not appreciating your new vibe.

Chapter 5

am I destined for failure?

"Failure" is a mindset, not an absolute. Every person who has become something has been challenged by denial. Frankly, every one of you reading this has faced "failure" because it comes in so many forms.

For example: being dumped, not getting a job, someone ignoring your plea, feeling left out etc...

We feel the emotions encompassing letdown and failure, even though we don't categorize them as such- we often label them as "frustration" or "sadness" without introspecting.

No one is destined for failure, but we all come onto Earth and reincarnate to face it. Accepting that fact is more manageable than resistance. You may be wondering how someone super rich is a failure because you have narrowed your mindset to success equalling financial freedom.

Wealthy people often make "ends meet" in their pockets. Those who do the healing work and commit to fulfilling their purpose are more likely to have a well-rounded life of success.

How many rich people are empty in the heart or have mediocre relationships with their families? Many.

So, we do need to remember that our circumstances reflect how we, as energy, chose and choose to show up on the planet. What did your soul choose to learn in this lifetime? Where were your hardships and struggles going to be? You are destined to find out—that is the guarantee (whether you do something about it is your choice!).

Remember the grid from earlier? That is how we gain perspective on all that is possible for us.

Failure can become a disease if we bathe in it instead of persevering. It isn't that we can't sulk or become sad about things not going as planned; it is more that we need to get back up to eventually achieve our goals.

Manifesting is not inaction; it is producing the right actions. If you are completely still and asking the Universe to provide, you will be waiting a long time. If you are moving in the direction of where you wish to be, then the Universe and your guides know that you are serious about achieving that which you think about.

You can dream about being a lawyer, doctor, or Cordon Bleu graduate... but how is that possible if you don't apply or check the prerequisites? The path after acceptance on your path isn't guaranteed to be smooth sailing - but being on that road will give you a chance to see how resilient you are.

There are a couple of different avenues for success.

1) The Path of Least Resistance
2) Working Hard for What you Want

The difference between the two is that you tend to learn more about what isn't making you drained once you go through the experience(s) of feeling worn out. Many people in the world, like creators, find a niche that they succeed in off the bat. But remember, that also takes a lot of work and time that we do not traditionally see.

Living a life of purpose will still take time, even if you enjoy doing it. So, when people get discouraged that their chosen vocation is different from what they thought - they may try to manifest something that takes zero effort. To live a life of no effort, you must mooch, be given intergenerational wealth (or a wealthy partner), or work hard to get it.

Sometimes, people win the lottery in life, and it could be because they have lived many lives of having nothing and are finally going to bask in the glory of being provided for without fighting for dear life.

Don't get jealous! If it's not now, it'll be one day.

-

Since we have parallel timelines, we have ample opportunity.

a)__________________ (a timeline where you fail); you can switch to b)_______________________________________+ (a timeline where you succeed)

It is about getting off of "a" and making the shift to "b"–the main way to do that is by shifting your mindset. Be mindful of what you consume and the stories you tell yourself. Your brain is so powerful that overthinking or pessimism will become how you act.

When you start affirming better, you will face how negative you may be. If you don't believe that "you are worthy" or "you are successful," your brain will keep you away from it. But... this will change the more you affirm positive things to yourself.

Your reality will shift based on how you perceive it.

On a scale of 1 to 10 (1 being easy, and 10 being super uncomfortable), how do you feel when you say these things outloud to yourself?

Come back in a few weeks and do it again. The key is to affirm these or similar quotes daily to release the programming of "fight or flight" or our egos protection.

DEBUNKING THE WORLD WE LIVE IN: UNPACKING THE MATRIX AND SYSTEM

Scale of 1-10

	Today	2 weeks	3 weeks	4 weeks
I am worthy	_____	_____	_____	_____
I am wealthy	_____	_____	_____	_____
I am loved	_____	_____	_____	_____
I am beautiful	_____	_____	_____	_____
I am protected	_____	_____	_____	_____
I am smart	_____	_____	_____	_____
I am powerful	_____	_____	_____	_____

As mentioned, write from 1 to 10 in the blank spots provided in those 2-4 week intervals to see how, where, and if your programming shifted. The area in life where you feel the most resistance is the area that requires the most exploration and healing.

-

DEBUNKING THE WORLD WE LIVE IN: UNPACKING THE MATRIX AND SYSTEM

It is important to remember that a lot of what we think is failure is internalization from being a child. We carry that trauma throughout life as a reminder of our vulnerability but also our power to heal. What seemed like small rejections, like being bullied once on a playground as an 8-year-old, forced into "time out" at a five-year-old, or getting an F on a test in grade 7 - are all memories that we held onto as what we thought was, "our value of self."

Those moments do not define us, but they sometimes show us our capacity to receive and feel love. Sometimes, we stop ourselves from expanding because those triggers are alive and/or unresolved within our nervous system. If we fear feeling the hurt we felt in those moments throughout life, we can put up a wall to "avoid failure," which eventually leads to living a sheltered, insecure, and neglected life.

We manifest hurt because we assume we are here to be disciplined or ridiculed. When we work on affirming better, we tell our inner child, our nervous system, and our brain that we are guaranteed (and deserving) of a life of happiness/love.

Combining the above with your intergenerational patterns, traumas, and connection(s) to your past lives should be enough to see why we are challenged in the 3D world.

-

You may get jealous seeing that some are succeeding and feel that you are not. This is usually an illusion. As mentioned above, it is about where in life one is succeeding. So many get caught up in celebrities, athletes, and influencers "making the bank," but they do not necessarily realize how much work goes into it.

Would you put your face, family, potential, and reputation on television or social media daily to be judged? Are you in a position to face death threats because you make money?

These are rhetorical questions.

Growing up, we idolized athletes. It doesn't mean they aren't successful, but they show us that creating a level of greatness and skill at something recognizable comes with the price of "being known." This level of notoriety is often a trade-off for the "court of public opinion," i.e., the world feels there is a "free for all" to judge them because there is a presence.

It is interesting how that works.

Sometimes, this is psychological. If we feel that there is a chance to project or minimize those who are "higher up" on a hypothetical food chain in society, it makes us feel better because we see them as more like us.

In reality, we all face these fears of failure and perception - life is about being grounded regardless of those facts.

-

What if you looked at your life like the globe? Could you hop onto a plane and get to the next destination? Maybe. Maybe not. It all depends on the level of belief within your programming or identity right now.

For example, if you leave from Vancouver to London - you may have a layover in Toronto. If you pay more, you could have a direct flight. Think of those destinations and points as periods of your manifestations. Layovers will give you a pause: a chance to regroup. It doesn't mean you aren't getting to where you want to go - you're just uncertain or waiting. If you pay more, you can get there faster: it may mean giving up mentalities or people who don't want you to get onto that flight.

Booking a flight or planning a trip is more straightforward or realistic because you know what you need to do. We do not have that faith in ourselves when it comes to energy, though. There is a strong resistance to living in the assumption of a future that we admire because we think we're not in receipt of the steps to achieve it. It is really a mindset.

If we can trust that our ability to manifest and our belief system(s) is enough to get us on the right track, then the Universe will give us the signs and syncs that we're on the path. They aren't going to hand it to you in bed the next morning like a concierge, but they will challenge you to put your pride aside and follow the necessary steps in tandem with their guidance.

Some people believe that everything that is meant will come within arms reach without lifting a finger. This is only possible if you're living in alignment. If you're asking to see the Golden Temple but you're sitting in a cubicle in Germany - you're going to get there once you legitimately take the steps to make it happen. It could be as simple as applying for vacation, finding a travel buddy, or researching how to get to Amritsar (where the Golden Temple is). If you're only busking away at emails, you'll only attract more emails and noise. It's about rationalizing and being a *doer.*

We are not "failures" because we are doers—we fail because we refuse to slow down and think about what we truly want to do.

There is magic and beauty in allowing life to show us what is truly necessary or help us feel good. If we are concerned about the ins and outs and start psyching ourselves out of manifesting, then we will probably continue to be guided down a rabbit hole until we start to realize that we are in an abyss.

Chapter 6

does one thing impact everything?

You may have noticed that the rest fall like dominoes when one thing happens.

There is a chain reaction from "something bad" to the next thing turning sour, too.

This is an energy transference. If you believe you can keep one aspect of your life solid while the rest matter less or dwindle, you'll have to think again!

Perhaps you don't even realize how it impacts you.

Energy is a timeline.

The below timeline graph is something I call "the energy timeline." Everything in life is connected, and how you feel about one topic of life eventually impacts one and then all topics. If you feel out of alignment with work, you'll start to feel out of alignment at home or with family.

Here are some examples:

- *You start to get mistreated at work and build up resentment in the office. Eventually, you come home exhausted and drained and distance yourself from your family, which creates relationship issues.*

- *Secrets about your life become normal, and you start a bad habit or coping mechanism. You find yourself telling "white lies" often, which leads to slipping up, being dishonest, and tarnishing relationships from work to friends, family, and maybe even your children.*

- *Cheating on your partner starts to become regular because you feel undervalued. You start doing this on your break at work, but you lose track of time on multiple occasions. You miss deadlines and eventually get fired. The very thing you tried to keep "out of the home" is the same thing that leads to financial issues and mistrust within.*

ENERGY IS A TIMELINE

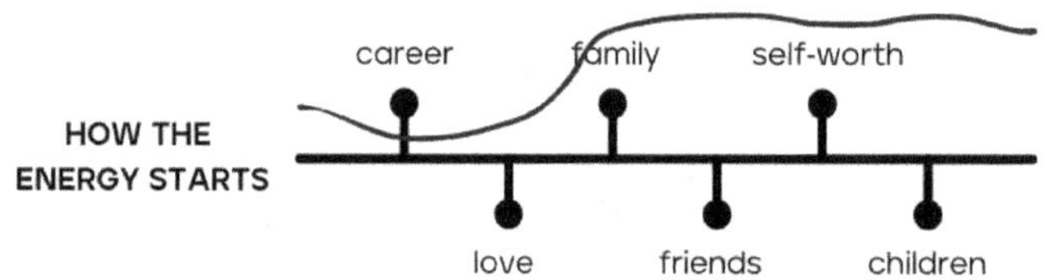

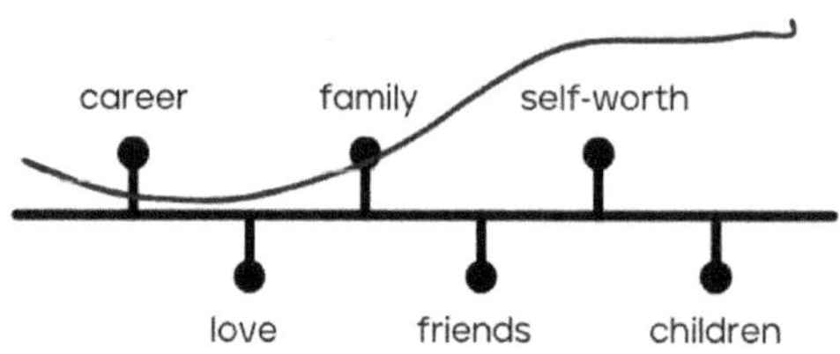

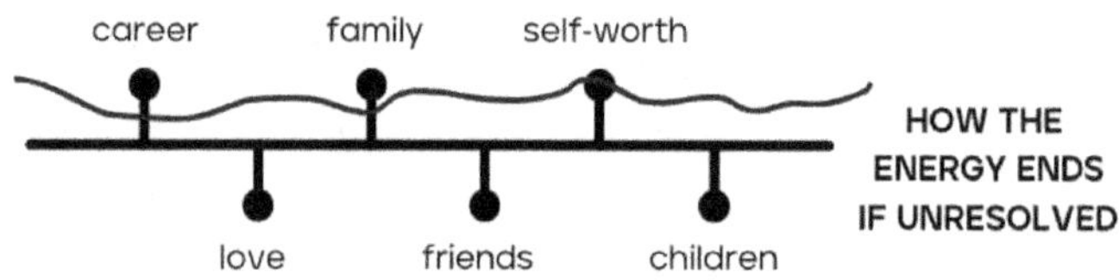

You can mix and match the categories. One will eventually trickle down into the other. Think of it cancer that spreads into other parts of the body.

If we can consciously realize and face the fact that our action, or inaction, is energetically connected to the outcomes we seek - then we can start to live a life of overall alignment. This shift in perspective may force you to make difficult decisions, but it promises a better trajectory if we face what is holding us back. Sometimes, this means partaking in those problematic conversations "off the bat" versus holding off and manifesting a bigger clusterf*ck.

We love to avoid things as humans! After time goes on, we hopefully realize that avoidance is the one thing that keeps us in a spiral of the same situation or outcomes.

By avoiding discussion, we detour around change. Avoidance allows things to fade, but it's essentially piling over unresolved issues, expectations, and patterns.

A doctor on TikTok once said that many doctors try to cover up the smell by prescribing heavier odour eliminators rather than teaching a patient to take the garbage out (i.e., keep taking this pill; the root cause doesn't matter). The same goes for energy. You can avoid and keep piling on top of the dumpster pile. Eventually, it'll turn into a fire you wished you had cleaned up sooner. Rather than piling issues on top of the pile, take that item (topic of conversation) and address it so that you can transmute it into something positive.

Nothing good ever comes from lowering your expectations of yourself and others.

We can only avoid accountability for healing certain parts of ourselves if we *completely* eliminate the possibility of them from our existence. For instance, we don't choose a life partner, say no to kids, or play it safe in any area.

-

We covered this a bit in a previous chapter, but the healing we do on ourselves helps heal those connected to us. When we decide to be better for ourselves, we allow people to do the same for themselves. If someone is not meant to be in our life, they will naturally fade away (permanently or temporarily). You aren't doing anything wrong; you are just manifesting and aligning with a different timeline, which is better for the manifestations you seek.

ENERGY BUBBLE

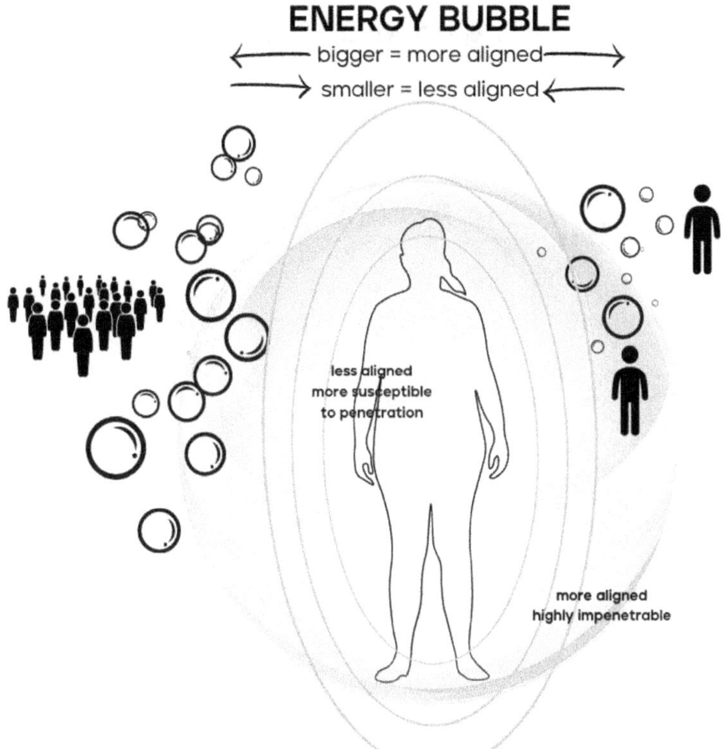

You let off positive energy bubbles the higher you vibrate (are in alignment). If you have negative energy, you can exude that too! As can others around you who are unaligned.

Some may see this as an "aura" which is also true.

ENERGY BUBBLE
healing generations

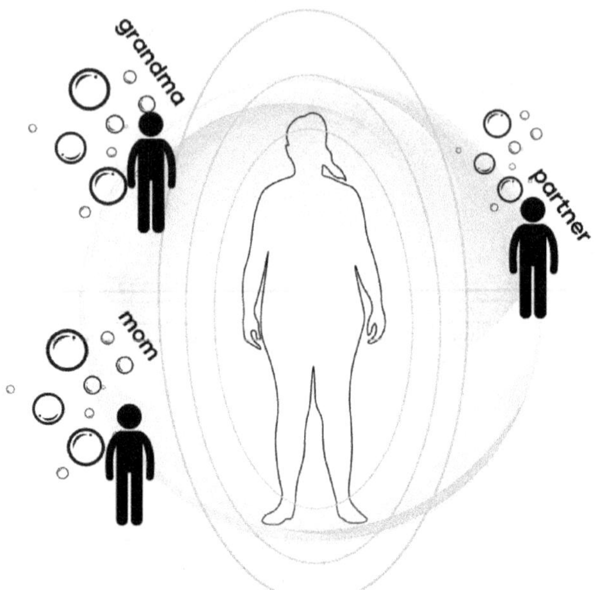

The higher you get in vibration, the more likely (not guaranteed) that you will heal family and partners around you. It doesn't matter that you're not blood related to your partner.

You can heal generational patterns like discussed before this.

I call this "the light bubble". We have a big bubble of energy that is like a light around us. This is available to us when we are acting from a place of alignment, gratitude, respecting our boundaries, and affirming all that is positive. This bubble around us lets off bubbles (as if you were blowing through a wand)... those bubbles can "pop light" onto those in your circle or even strangers on the street. This happens when you live purposefully, and others around you will be inspired to act according to the same principles because they're starting to feel more light around them. This light could give them a spiritual download, feel energetically refined, motivated, loved, etc...

Our "light bubble" needs to be protected at all times. We have to make it impenetrable. This can be hard to do at the beginning because below are the things required to do that (or at least make you less susceptible to interference, which is the "penetration"):

- Lack of boundaries
- Doing unaligned activities
- Saying yes to things that are a no
- Unhealthy habits
- Not committing to your path
- Refusing to speak your truth/avoidance
- Anything else along those lines. There is no absolute list.

People will inevitably want to "penetrate your bubble" when you live an authentic life. It may sound like a funny term, but it's the truth. Look at the people around you as needles.

The above shows you the way in which people will try to "get in your space." Some people do this on purpose, whereas others do it unconsciously. You can determine this by seeing whether people respect you for asserting your stance on certain things. If people keep asking you to do something you've been uncomfortable with, they likely have their own avoidant or trauma pattern, or they simply want you to validate them. It may not be too harmful, but it can cause a considerable ripple in your energy and alignment, which dims your bubble. Others do it without

realizing they are because they are programmed to please people (which has them assume that you will do the same).

"People-pleasing" behaviours will always dim your light and penetrate your energy bubble.

-

If people continuously try infiltrating your space, you'll be in for a long ride. When boundaries are not put in place, this could be a lifelong thing. This "seeping" of your impermeability will be like a balloon that slowly deflates. You'll eventually look, feel, and perform differently when you have a hole in your space.

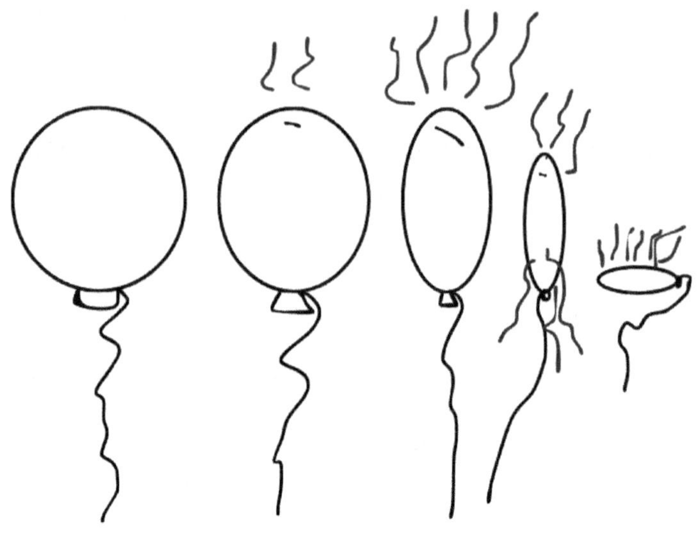

The infiltration is similar to the needles in terms of topics. If there are continuous jabs in your space, then you will eventually have to make the decision to patch things up, or deplete energy. If this happens continuously, then you won't even be able to see where the holes are as you'll be completely burn out or deflated. Think about when a balloon loses helium over time.

The balloons above show you how the "air," which is your own light, dissipates over time. You can patch the hole by resetting your boundaries, but you'll eventually be left without anything if you do not. This is how burnout occurs.

We all hate "burnout"! Why would we intentionally put ourselves in that position?

The ability to burn out (or use all of your energy) is linked to your intuition. If you refuse to do the work to create safety around you, you'll start utilizing your energy to please others or work against yourself.

For example, if you avoid taking time off because you don't want your boss to hate you, you'll choose to build codependency in your workplace over your mental health.

Ignoring your healthy expectations in a relationship to avoid conflict can lead to more significant issues.

There are many opportunities to avoid burnout, but we are programmed not to use them because "we are selfish." You are not selfish; you are providing the energy to yourself that others cannot provide to you—this is what I refer to as "the orbit."

THE ORBIT

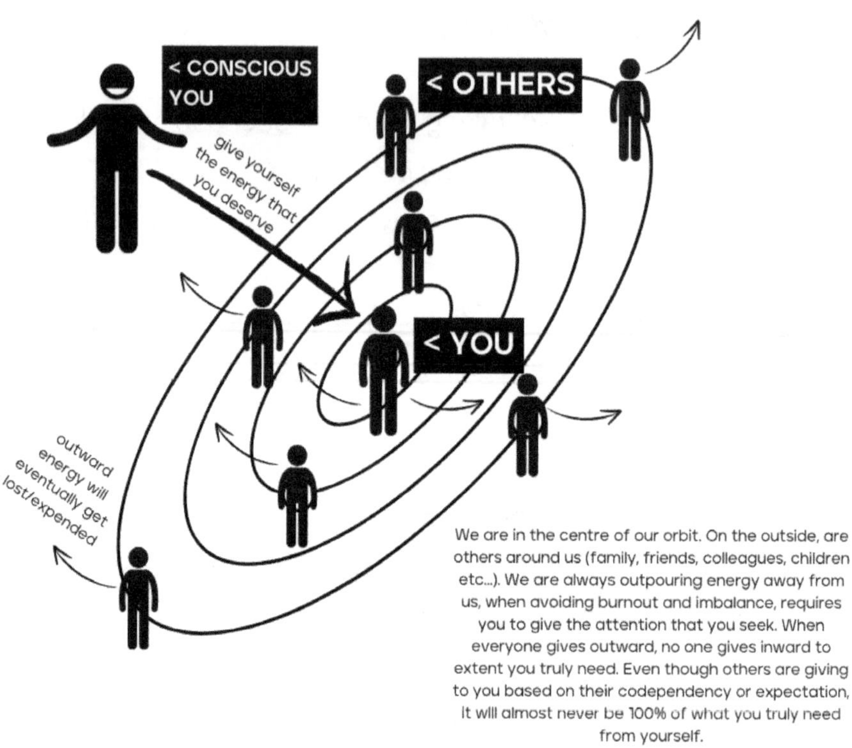

We are in the centre of our orbit. On the outside, are others around us (family, friends, colleagues, children etc...). We are always outpouring energy away from us, when avoiding burnout and imbalance, requires you to give the attention that you seek. When everyone gives outward, no one gives inward to extent you truly need. Even though others are giving to you based on their codependency or expectation, It will almost never be 100% of what you truly need from yourself.

The orbit is where your energy is extended. We may continue to give energy outward in the hopes that someone will eventually give it to us, too. Since we are all giving, no one is receiving. This is why it is necessary to give love and care to ourselves so that we feel fulfilled without relying on others for that.

This is the time to take back your power. You were told that power was meant to be given to those around you. What did that do but create codependent patterns? We need to rely on ourselves rather than others. This is also how you break generational patterns.

Allowing ourselves to make decisions that are different from those of our ancestors in potentially more vulnerable or narrow-minded environments (which could honestly just be selfishness or righteousness) breaks the pattern of expectation for those after us. It also gives your friends and/or family permission to make decisions that align with their passion(s). If you're willing to do what you need to do for yourself, and you have the privilege and ability to do so, then others will follow suit.

You just need to be accountable for giving others that option - including your own children, etc.... so that they do not fall into the same trap.

-

These decisions that are made are also rooted in our past lives. We are given opportunities in our present life to overcome the challenges that held us back in the past. Being open to new experiences and allowing discomfort means we are destined for something better. Something may be unaligned rather than outright "horrible" to you. The discomfort we feel (especially when very

intense) can indicate that the steps you're making are something you have not done before. This is particularly true when you are following your intuition.

If you are taking steps that you regret or disagree with, then you will know—but that's not what we are talking about here.

Intense emotions, burning sensations in your gut, or anxiousness can be a sign that you are transcending into a whole new lifestyle—one that you have not been able to experience due to hardships, trauma, and/or restrictions in one or more past lives.

Imagine reincarnating with wealth or a fantastic job, but your energy remembers being poor. This would make it difficult for you to make investment decisions, even though you wouldn't "go broke." These resistances you are overcoming are helping your energy gain new strength and resilience.

It is not a punishment.

Chapter 7

how our past lives impact our current one

Unless you live or learn in a spiritual environment, past lives and their impact on our current lives are something you are not taught. If you're reading this book, that means you've likely had multiple past lives. How do I know that? Because you would not be at a level of consciousness to absorb this material. Ego blocks you from learning about spirituality, and allowing yourself to learn means you are open to change. When you're entirely unwilling, you have a lot to learn, which means that you are at the beginning stages of your incarnations on Earth.

We continue returning to Earth because of the things left to learn. This is something that I refer to as "dilution," similar to intergenerational patterns and/or trauma.

DILUTION

The above diagram shows how you may have different lessons with the same emotional or physical responses. You continue returning to 3D life because your soul wants to "get better" and more advanced. You eventually learn so much that you reincarnate as a spiritual being, a healer in any regard, and then, after many lifetimes, will graduate into energy. NB: You will know when it is your last lifetime as your guides have ways to tell you. There is no escaping growth. You will be met with ways to fulfill the lesson, or you'll return to face it again.

Another way to tune into past lives is to remember the moments when you felt something but couldn't figure out why. You had a familiarity, a strong sense, or a deep understanding of the meaning. Did you know that you bring over wisdom from past lives? You pass through lifetimes with knowledge and lessons. There is a mutual benefit.

You can also consider this with "deja vu." Deja Vu is a remembrance of a specific timeline or parallel lifetime that you have been in. Sometimes, this dream comes to fruition in "real-time." Note that dreams are messages from your Spirit guides, and often, you will see the future in them. That "ah, this feels eerily familiar" is a notion of recalling your true sense of power in this lifetime and previous ones.

As mentioned previously, intense discomfort can be a sign that you are not in the scenario you are coming into or a sign that you have a chance to deal with it differently. If your energy does not remember being in a space of staying true to yourself, then "playing big" versus small will make you uncomfortable. If the energy in your current and past lives is used to the scenarios you are in, then you'll be calibrated to that comfort zone.

DEBUNKING THE WORLD WE LIVE IN: UNPACKING THE MATRIX AND SYSTEM

The diagram above shows you how you will feel when you make changes that make you uncomfortable. This <u>does not mean</u> you should put yourself in unsafe situations like abuse, assault, or disrespect. There is a vast difference between being uncomfortable when in alignment and your intuition agreeing that a place is fundamentally unsafe.

Some examples of when it is healthy to be uncomfortable and work through the lessons and past life experiences:

- You have been undervalued at a job and want to quit even though you don't know your next steps.

- There is a big decision to make in a relationship, and even though your lips quiver when you're advocating, you know you are standing up for yourself.

- Opportunities to be in a high-value environment are presented to you, and you feel nervous because it's something you haven't done before.

-

These feelings and insights are strongly available to children known as "indigo" or "conscious" children. Children who are not conditioned in this lifetime (or ones who are coming back after many lessons have been learned) will give you hints about who they are if you listen closely. That "meaningless conversation" about how your child lives in _____ or remembering when they worked as a _____ - is not made up. Those are indications of the lives that they lived before coming back to Earth.

Similarly, if you feel or have felt a connection to certain places or people, it is likely because you have had past lives in those areas or reincarnated into a lifetime with someone that you know from before.

That familiarity with friends, partners, and family is a sign that you have met them before. Your sibling could have been a partner; your parent could have been a sibling. This doesn't mean you are incestuous; you have a connection and bond that fits the relationship in this lifetime. The lessons may also reincarnate, or you may be given the option to "balance out karma." For example, if you reincarnate with a partner that you cheated on in a past life, they may do it in this life. The 3d world is a brutal teacher.

A "ripple effect" moves through the world's energy without us immediately processing the full details. The places we visit, the people we meet, where we study, the emotions we feel, etc.... are all tied with invisible strings through Earth. You may have heard of "the invisible string theory," a sequence of events leading you to someone you are destined to meet. Reflect on your life and how you have been connected through "bridges" of people or events. You'll be surprised!

Sometimes, you will see that you travelled to the same place at the same time as your husband, that you have many mutual friends from different groups with your wife, or that you attended the same school as your husband.

These are also known as the: "bridge of incidences".

BRIDGE OF INCIDENCES

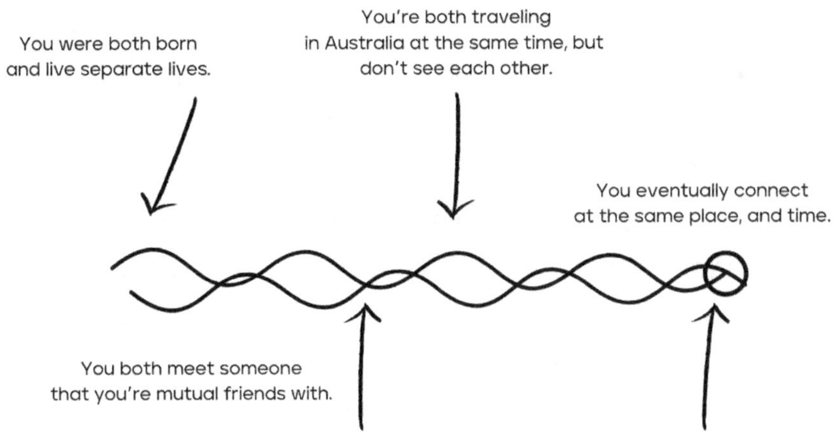

The above will briefly show how you are connected before you anticipate knowing someone. You often pick up on the energy or leave your energy (like a smell) to allow for an expansion into something you manifested. If aligned, you and another individual can bounce off one another like "bubbles" previously discussed. This will keep you on the timeline of showing up in each others' lives "for real".

You are also able to meditate to visit your past lives. Any person connected to themselves spiritually (or on a conscious level) can see what is called "the Akashic records" to unlock a part of their soul. Think of your soul as a Horcrux (if you are into Harry Potter). A Horcrux is not evil in this instance; it is pieces of you spread out through different timelines which have brought you to where you are today. You can gather this information to make more sense of your current circumstances. They are to be honoured and not destroyed. There will always be something that you can learn from your past, and your soul will always try to take you there.

Options to hold onto your lesson while knowing better after life experience is a powerful way to interact and transcend. You have likely been guided to places where your past lives (or a life) took place already, be it a travel destination, research on a destination, or a type of cuisine. The resonance with anything in the trilogy is an unlocking of a core memory that your soul carries in energetic form.

"How you can find out about past lives" is probably something on your mind. Here are some ways:

- Book a past-life reading.

- Look up my guided meditation on YouTube under "the RKH" to unlock your Akashic records.

- Ask your spirit guides and/or ancestors to show you signs of your past lives

-

It is easy for anyone to assume that their visions or spiritual "downloads" and insights are fake or made up. That is how our mind gets the best of us. If we ask for a sign of something and receive it - the trust is in accepting that it is real. That is one of the most complex parts of staying in tune with your spiritual abilities. Once you trust that the guidance and imagery you are receiving are real, you can begin to use it to discern. Note: this is not the case when you receive intrusive or anxious thoughts or someone telling you to do something dangerous. Always make sure to talk to a medical professional if you feel there is a mental health concern.

Our spirit guides won't intentionally lead us into or onto a dangerous path, but they will show you the ways in which your mindset has held you back. They will highlight certain patterns and behaviours that you have carried on from previous lives that are currently keeping you stuck. They may show you certain relationships and how they are impacting you. As mentioned before, you bring in relationships that your soul remembers and recognizes as a way to continue your healing journey. Some things are preordained into your karma.

It is expected that you will feel curious or even guilty about how you are more connected to one person than another, especially if it is a child or a grandchild. Remember that you have likely reincarnated with this relationship as part of a soul contract yet to be fulfilled.

But, what is a "soul contract"?

These are commitments that you make on your path to purpose. As humans, we come back to graduate and excel. This means that our relationships are also meant to join this new level. Whether that means investing more in meaningful connections or learning lessons from those who trigger us, we may be bonded more to specific individuals, but there is nothing wrong with that.

Did you know that you feel similar triggers in a romantic partnership as you did with your parent? For example, if you are a heterosexual woman who chooses a man, it is natural that that man would bring out wounds within you that are meant to be healed. This wounding would have been implanted through the interactions with your dad more specifically, but it will bring up experiences with any parent or guardian.

This is because we are set to heal our inner traumas. That is why we are here. Whether or not a relationship makes it "to the end" depends on both peoples' ability to heal these timelines, do the inner work, and create boundaries through reflection. This doesn't mean that you should stay in unhealthy relationships, but it does go to show the <u>way</u> that once-toxic dynamics can turn around with remorse, empathy, and reflection. It's all about the individual experience.

If or when we grow up in a healthy household without any of these dangerous dynamics, we are less likely to be required to heal many toxic patterns—mainly because we would have in many previous lives.

We are a reflection of the environment in which we grew up. Even if we see that everything was outwardly normal, we may feel certain pain, which brings about surprising yet triggering experiences (whether from our current lifetime as children or a past life pattern that has come to dilution).

Some of this is also carried through the intergenerational patterns discussed before.

-

Many of you have come back on this planet to be spiritual teachers, healers, and way-showers because you were not entirely given a chance before. Reincarnation at this specific moment in time is no coincidence. Millions of conscious souls were stifled in their ability to help Earth grow during orchestrated wars, famines, oppression, discrimination, and more.

We are sitting here today with the privilege of open dialogue and discussion because there is an actual chance to make a change and speak about issues which were once a legitimate cause of getting you killed. That is not an exaggeration.

If you are a healer or a thought leader and you feel anxiety about speaking up (or have), know that you are getting out of your comfort zone bubble. It is how you know that your body is excelling beyond what was seen to be acceptable and into a space of advocating for what you truly believe is needed– which is empathy.

Remember that the system was created to suffocate empathy and understanding.

Being here now means that you have the option (even when it is tough) to get your message out there without assuming you will lose your life like you would have in a past life because of healers and paganists being "burned at the stake" or persecuted.

Chapter 8

spiritualists are labelled satanists

We discussed this a bit before, but there should be a constant reminder that spirituality is not the root of evil—it is the eliminator of it. The reason that labels are put on individuals with holistic practices is that the system knows that those who can transcend have the ability to see the truth.

The truth is that we each have the power to make it through hardship on our own. The programming we have been ingesting since childhood has been intentional - unless we had parental figures or leaders who understood the importance of teaching us about our inner guidance system.

Why would the system want us to know that we have the power to know all? It would leave billionaires without the

power they continue to have over vulnerable citizens of
Earth, especially in the West.

The more spiritual places on Earth, like India or the Middle
East, have been infiltrated by colonizers who want to keep
people submissive. They want those who know their spiritual
essence to be vulnerable and poor. If they had the
resources to spread their message(s) and practice(s) far and
wide, then we would have a vast majority of "zen" people
across the planet.

Ever notice how the West has taken modalities from other
places rooted in spirituality and turned them into a colonial
business? Yoga, herbs+spices, energy drinks etc... The
names are chosen to manipulate and program individuals
into believing that the West "knows what they're talking
about" when it is about tricking you into not doing your
research about the origins. It is to keep you ignorant, naive,
and reliant.

The system is built to give you the "trust" (programming)
that what it teaches must be accurate and factual.

This is also why conscious children must be protected at all
costs. You may have heard that "children are our biggest

teachers or Gurus"–that has to be respected by every one of us for us to have a brighter future.

They have come back to promote consciousness with the purest intentions.

-

"Satan" is an intense word, but it is meant to get your attention.

Matrix and systemic programming are based on keeping people in formation. Anybody who tries to tell you that you do not have to be in a particular formation will be: shadow banned, censored, "misinformed", a "hippy" or "woohoo" and/or labelled as unreliable or "satan".

Isn't it interesting that the system can know every possible fact, but no one can question it? This is why so many people were ostracized during the "plandemic" (what I refer to the covid 19 epidemic as). We are now at the place where we have information and resources to question what is fed to us.

That's the thing: The system wants to feed you and give you no access to a different appetite. The menu is curated to give you a basic grasp of reality–something good enough to keep your curiosity at bay.

When you start to explore, travel, and invest in more information - "cuisines" - you realize how sh*t the West has become in their mindset. This is also why many have shifted to remote online work or building their own brands.

No one wants to be wholly reliant and/or in "golden handcuffs"!

A refresher on those handcuffs is that you will trust what you can rely on.

THE GOLDEN HANDCUFFS

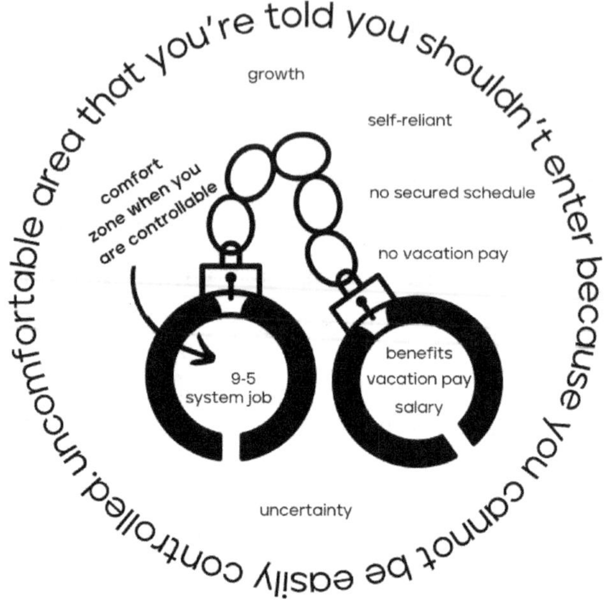

The description above is meant to show you how people stay stuck in handcuffs. The outside of them is difficult to accept because you want to have what is inside—similar to the comfort zone. The system doesn't want to empower you to be on the outside of the handcuffs because it doesn't have control over you. Millions of people rely purely on the system because every institution they are a part of is in that systemic vortex and reprogramming the same message whenever or wherever possible.

DEBUNKING THE WORLD WE LIVE IN: UNPACKING THE
MATRIX AND SYSTEM

-

A part of the programming that the system and matrix want to plant on you is that you are unable to make the best decisions for yourself. It's like a parent. When a parent asserts demand or knowledge against you, you'll grow up believing it is in your best interest. The reflection as you deprogram when you get older will show you where your trauma lies.

But why are we designed this way?

This is our human design, our soul's blueprint from birth. It is how we make decisions and are created to be in alignment. The system blocks those **"portals of activation"**, as I like to call them.

It isn't that spirit doesn't love us - it's that we signed up to play a particular game. We must accept that at some point.

Our energy is also programmed into our human design for the positive. Our design is implanted within us and holds all of the knowledge that we are meant to learn throughout life. Our personality also plays a part, but it is something that we are more conscious of.

We uncover our design by asserting our personality.

Some of our traumas are also built into us through intergenerational patterns and what our soul's "algorithm" wants us to know. A lot of this is placed within our gates in human design. I call those "the portals of activation."

The reason is that we are all meant to "light up" in the gates of our lives that are an inherent part of us. We are told that we must be good at everything, but we are not built that way. This leads to burning out.

Teaching yourself about your human design will give you that option. You can get started via my free and extension guides on my website (www.therkh.com).

Your design is where you'll also see more about your purpose. **Purpose is a way you act; it is not a destination**. It is the way your spirit wants you to carry yourself on a daily basis. Doing these actions and living in that fulfillment will guide your direction and manifestations in life.

DEBUNKING THE WORLD WE LIVE IN: UNPACKING THE MATRIX AND SYSTEM

If you knew it was as easy as acting a certain way, you would have been successful without the system telling me you need a pedigree to be "worthy".

-

People spend their whole lives wanting to know how to succeed, but investing in the experience of finding out can be daunting. This can happen because we set high expectations to know everything about ourselves, but we need to realize that life is a continuous journey.

Your design is meant to tell you about how you are challenged and in which ways your body is informed to be more productive.

The system relies on your dependence on them - even when you burn out. Your depletion is assumed to be "failure", or you "didn't do things good enough" - when really, your environment is unaligned for you. Asking for your worth, value, and time in those moments is scary because:

1) Value is underappreciated in the system if it is run by those who have programming;

2) Your anxiety is so far deep within you, and by the time you feel better, you will be back on the cycle.

Think of it as the time you stopped feeling nauseous after a tumultuous roller coaster—only to get on the next ride to start all over again. The key is getting off the ride altogether, knowing that you are not missing out on anything.

-

Think of your value as "satanic energy" in the matrix. This is because you have spent much of your life conditioned to believe that standing up for yourself is wrong. Having people in your corner who advocate for you is a gift that has been hard to come by until now. When you are a people-pleaser and lack boundaries, you are seen as an "angel". That's because people want to use you as a way to feel better about themselves. You asserting your worth is something that triggers those who do not have self-worth or the perspective to look beyond the lens of their own experience(s).

For instance, you are meant to feel a full-body " yes" when it comes to taking on any experience. But... how many times

have you said yes when it is really a "no"? What did it do
to your body, mental health, and emotional capacity?

If you shrunk yourself or felt tired and irritated, that is a sign
that you stepped out of alignment. The interesting thing
about humankind is that people around you will want
an excuse for why it's a "no" rather than taking your intuition
as a valid justification. We are programmed to have reasons
and explanations, and moving away from that will make you
feel selfish when you are <u>in the wrong crowd.</u>

It's difficult when that "wrong crowd" are people that you are
used to being around. The trade-off is asserting your
boundary and limiting your explanations until the recipients
understand that you will not waver on what is best for you.

-

One way we can stop these cycles from happening is by
empowering the children around us to learn about their
guidance system earlier in life. This technically falls on their
parents and guardians to enforce. It also means that those
individuals will need to address their limiting beliefs,
boundaries, and self-worth to ensure the children get what
they need.

We often see a child's boundaries as something offensive.

Everyone needs to realize and appreciate that a child's opinion is unfiltered and not meant to appease you. Over time, they are told that they are wrong and then revert to "people-pleasing" if convinced that they should choose what makes another feel validated. This is why people, "on the spectrum" are more free-spirited and opinionated - it's also how trauma can and will start, and it will build up resentment, which opens up for healing later in life.

Some examples:

> - A child doesn't want to hug somebody. Adults see it as "rude", whereas the child doesn't feel safe or aligned with the energy. Society must stop promoting this boundary as a lack of respect for elders.

> - Your preteen started an activity and wants to switch frequently... There is a fine balance between being non-committal and disciplined and staying in an unaligned environment. The child's human design may have been switching between environments, experiences, and hobbies because they are taking

what they need and then outgrowing a place after they have received it. This can naturally be frustrating and will require teamwork to see the best way to implement structure and routine.

- If your kid doesn't want to try new foods, they may be labelled as "too picky" or ungrateful. Their past-life energy may also play into what they like. For example, if they're simple, they could have lived in poverty in a past life. For many, their design is tailored to structure and having a predictable diet - that is how they're more successful and aligned. Try new ways of incorporating different foods while making them feel safe with what they know.

Some may see the above as "enabling," but it is not. The enabling is for the parent, guardian, or person forcing someone to do something against their guidance system. There is no cookie-cutter formula. Trusting that a lack of appreciation is not the reason that people make decisions will give many a chance to reflect on how everyone is living their own experience.

Labels are meant to keep you small while skirting around empathy.

DEBUNKING THE WORLD WE LIVE IN: UNPACKING THE MATRIX AND SYSTEM

-

Many equate confidence to arrogance. While this can be true, it usually isn't the motive. Having a sense of worth automatically means you are confident. That confidence to assert means you will be judged by those who either do not see it in themselves or who want you to be a malleable player within the system.

The system can also promote mindsets. Getting away from those mindsets can result in a lot of ego-crushing —ironic how that can happen when you have a false sense of confidence. The reason this happens is that confidence of this type is arrogance, which is masking insecurity. The moment you start to unravel the thread of the root of those emotions is when you will actually start to see the value of people around you. It helps you have confidence with courage.

The mindsets mentioned include affirmative thought processes. This can consist of empathizing, wishful thinking, favourable outcomes, expecting positivity, etc... The system will tell you that those things can only be provided to you through their confirmation.

This is not true.

When people start to talk about shifting their minds to create new labels like "demonic energy" or "foo foo" are blasted through the algorithm to gaslight individuals who know it is the truth.

Therefore, people integrating onto a new path may question whether they need to be more informed or feel better.

-

Remember that trusting your inner voice is never going to lead you astray. It may temporarily cause you to have some fractures in your trilogy, but it will not be forever. You will start to be grateful when you start to see the light that comes from becoming spiritually aligned.

The matrix has programmed through the system to trust your mind over your heart and guidance system. It will take time to unpack that - but you can and will.

Chapter 9
finding meaning

We like to believe that it is impossible to create our reality - but it isn't!

How you manifest what you want is based on how you associate it with your power. Those who think they are limited in opportunity are the same people who "play small." If you want to "be big", you need to act accordingly.

Your reality adjustment is strongly based on your surroundings. Who are you talking to? What is your motivation? How do you feel daily? If these factors make you feel "worse" rather than better, then it is time to change your daily life. Using the information throughout this book will hopefully allow you to do that with more awareness.

Change is hard. There could be a small daily habit that is difficult to change but lends the most significant result(s) in the long term. Perhaps you make a "big cut" of a friendship that only involves your alignment, and it improves your output of energy. Remember that all these adjustments will keep you in alignment and happier.

There are several reasons why you may find it challenging to make the changes; perhaps because you're:

- Afraid of what people will think.
- Scared.
- Uncertain.
- Uncomfortable or comfortable.
- A people-pleaser.

- _______________

- _______________

- _______________

- _______________

- _______________

Feel free to fill the lines in with your own reflection/words.

Do you see how the above terms and conditions are not really because of your lack of faith in it working out?

If you knew it would work out, you'd do it automatically.

-

How can you do it automatically? Well, this takes a lot of practice, patience, and perseverance. You must know that it will not and cannot happen overnight. This is because you will have to reframe your mindset and intentions—and this takes time. If you are doubtful, getting to "super hopeful" or grateful most of the time will be a massive reintegration for you.

There are so many people regardless of their spiritual path and alignment who lack faith in things working out.

If your dominant thought is that "nothing is working out for me," then the Universe cannot give you the opposite. You have to trust your mind as if it were a computer.

What are you feeding it? It will give you the same.

POSITIVE THOUGHTS

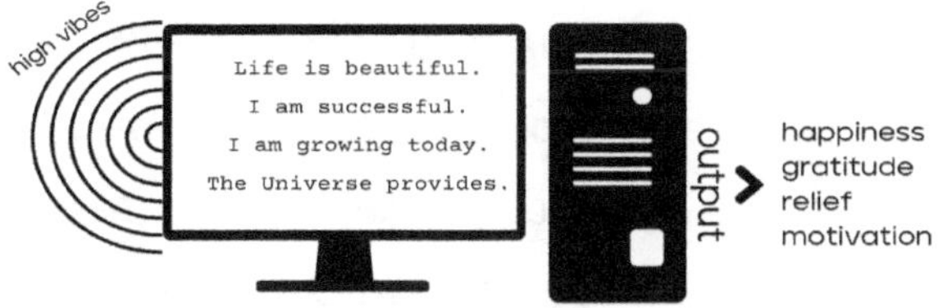

NEGATIVE THOUGHTS

The above diagram shows the difference in thought processes and what you gain from them. Are you continuously "down" on yourself and overheating your computer with doubt? Or are you allowing yourself to upgrade it with positive thoughts so that it can give you those things?

-

Everyone should focus on "the little things" to shift their reality. This could be gratitude for moments you take for granted, ongoing appreciation, or looking at how far you have come.

DEBUNKING THE WORLD WE LIVE IN: UNPACKING THE
MATRIX AND SYSTEM

One of the most profound ways to see life differently is by acknowledging that where you are now is somewhere you once wished to be. It is hard to see the progression when we live 3d life slowly - especially when the emotions are something we feel fully or consistently.

Some examples:

- You were seeking a fulfilling relationship, and life changed so fast once you found the person that you forgot to acknowledge that you once wished for it.

- There were limiting beliefs holding you back, and you forgot that it was hard to conquer them now that life has improved.

- A dream job opportunity came on your doorstep, and you've been so busy "living through it" that you missed that a paycheque was once a dream and not expected.

It is important to see the beauty in the little things in life—the moments you feel heat or see the lights on at home, when you have Wi-Fi to work on or browse with, a warm meal from an oven, or the luxury of going to the store and picking out what you want or need.

For many of you, these were once things that you struggled to have (or didn't know how to maintain). We shouldn't be scared to go back there, but feeling gratitude for this lifestyle is something that we should hold onto.

Some of these "gratitude moments" are more potent and resonant with individuals who have established lifestyle boundaries. Perhaps you moved out of a family home to have mental, energetic, physical, and emotional space. This may have been hard initially, and you could have struggled.

When you are in a manifestation but feeling confined, focus on why you have done what you did. One of the reasons it is more complex than you may have thought is because you are ridding yourself of old lifestyles, beliefs, codependency, and routines. Breaking away will mean that you will have more time to reflect.

Nothing worth having and deserving comes easy. Be kind to yourself. You can start by looking at what you are grateful for in your surroundings (s) today.

-

A lot of the time, we forget that we are in control of our life circumstances. Sure, there are important links and relationships within the trilogy - but it doesn't mean that they should impact our ability to achieve what we seek.

Giving power external to us will keep us in a constant loop of external validation - as discussed with the orbit. The reality we want to manifest is only available with our action steps. No one will force us to make those changes unless they have done the inner work to find their power.

Typically, we do this on our own.

It's essential to evaluate the pros and cons of our lives consistently. Are you feeling good or bad about the trilogy surrounding you? Is there something you can adjust to feel more in alignment?

The reason you have to do the test of the above on your own is so you can answer the questions honestly.

-

Here are some questions to ask yourself:

If I could eliminate someone from my life to feel better, is there anyone it would be?

____

____

What in my life is draining my energy right now?

____

____

How do I feel about my career?

____

____

Am I fulfilling my purpose?

____

____

Where is there room for improvement in my life?

____

____

The above is not meant to keep you focused on the negative but to give you some routine questions to consider when you're feeling ungrounded, in reflection mode, or just considering your next steps.

*If the trilogy has a revolving door that triggers you, then you may see why or how you're magnetizing to certain patterns. Assess the pros and cons of it thoroughly.

-

DEBUNKING THE WORLD WE LIVE IN: UNPACKING THE MATRIX AND SYSTEM

Giving yourself the grace to make significant changes is going to take work. Taking those first steps will be a feat because this could be the first time you are in a position to do that. That also has change feeling scary.

Have you taken a cold plunge? Or "ripped a bandaid off" in a situation? It eventually gets easier as you know what to expect. You will become more resilient and familiar with the changes, which automatically leads you to create more space for alignment in your life.

Whether we jump straight into the deep end or gradually move from the shallow end and beyond, our guides will make sure that the support we need is in place. It won't be as simple as a referee or lifeguard guiding our every move, but you will feel the omnipresence as you start to encounter and integrate relief into your nervous system.

At the beginning of any significant change, you'll feel very nervous, anxious, and sad. Knowing it's for the right reasons does not negate the need to "catch up" to any shift. This is what I call the hollow conduit. It is when we transition into the new while dealing with the abyss.

The hollow conduit is our energy field when we are in the middle of significant life changes. We feel a sense of unknown, confusion, hesitation, and a looming look into the abyss of our lives. We feel empty and confused because we have allowed the old to shed and are waiting for the new to still "land" into our bodies.

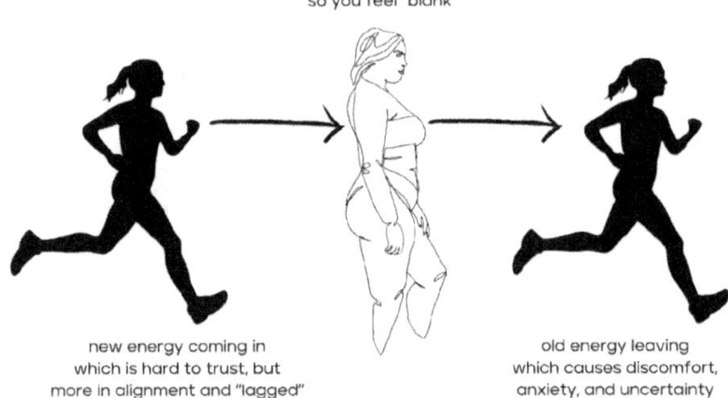

The above representation shows us how new energy catches up behind us after we let go of the old energy. There is a lag between the old leaving and the latest coming, which leaves us feeling hollow and looking for direction. It is essential to stay strict and structured with yourself at this time, as it is when

many people revert to old behaviours and patterns within the trilogy to avoid discomfort and/or uncertainty.

Eventually, the processing time feels trivial. It does not matter because there is a sense of belonging, familiarity, and comfort in trusting that what was once unknown will become clarified–usually after having experienced this transition a couple of times.

We can reincarnate into our body. The "phoenix rising" energy allows for transformation(s), which keeps us growing and resilient. We can shed the old skin of who we were while grieving that version of us that gave birth to a new transformation. "Ego death" or dread may resonate too.

This is like giving birth to yourself all over again. During these moments, you must be kind and gentle to your soul and body. Rest becomes very important as you will be challenged to remain still when planting new manifestations. The reason is that you cannot keep running away while expecting something to catch up.

The above shows how you can actually keep a manifestation away from you if you are unwilling to take a breather, pause, or rest day to allow it in. If the manifestation and new energy are behind you, you must allow them to meet you. They will not speed up to do so unless you give them the chance to acclimate to your vibe. The run tends to be a coping mechanism to avoid failure or the fear of something not panning out.

One of the worst things you can force yourself to do during this reincarnation is more! If you are a new person in energetic form, what makes you think that you don't need time to grow into that person? Sometimes, it is helpful to think of the "new you" as a newborn or infant. You would not force a two-week-old baby to run, let alone walk.

We must be mindful of how much we try to control our process. You may have heard that you're in charge of the what and why in your manifestation, and the Universe controls the how and when.

You will get what you seek if your intentions are pure.

Conclusion

I am sure that reading this was a lot. Whether you know any or all of this or are learning some for the first time… there is no doubt that completing and making it here is a reprogramming and shift for your subconscious. You will start to see the world differently now. It will keep you aware of how the trilogy impacts you, as well as how you impact others.

I am sure you will re-address and reinterpret several instances. Do not be hard on yourself during these times. It is natural to have a lifelong process of growing—that's in your human design, as we talked about.

You are not meant to know everything about yourself in one shot.

If you were, you wouldn't be reincarnating to come back here and experience Earth multiple times. The moment you truly sink into the fact that you are ever-growing and evolving, you will know that you are ascending into higher dimensions and levels of consciousness.

The beauty of accepting that everybody is on their timeline and that each of our healing is in conjunction with divine alignment should help us avoid blaming those around us. It is natural to seek accountability or have concerns and judgement; we cannot ignore that - but we can control whether we allow that to feed our requirement for empathy. The more you heal, the more you grow and realize that peoples' actions reflect their experience, not necessarily a slight at those around them.

You probably cannot count the times you have been judged or felt it. The stress of people-pleasing starts to fade as you appreciate and absorb how the world was made and why.

Having the chance to think about our biases and programming and shift our mindset is a privilege we have from the environments we grew up in. If we were given the space to open up our thoughts, we could shift and become the highest version of ourselves (even if we create that space ourselves).

Trusting that people around us will make us that version of ourselves is not something to rely on. We must believe and work toward being that confidant. Why? Because we are the only ones that we can control; therefore, we can't rely on others to do it in perpetuity.

So, I leave you with this:

If there was one lesson that you can start on from this book, what is it? How can you change your current reality with the trilogy to live a life of more alignment? Take out a pen/paper or your phone with a notes app and write/type what comes to mind.

You will be surprised how things change next.

Thank you for joining me on this self-exploration journey. I am proud of you!

Love, Rami - the RKH.

Appendix

Abyss: this is the energetic space of confusion and the void that you feel when there is uncertainty about what is coming next. It is the process of time between you affirming your manifestation to the universe, and actually receiving it.

Grid: the grid is the timelines that we live on which are often parallel to one another. This is because one decision can change our life. Knowing you have opportunities to jump forward into something better is the benefit of acknowledging the grid.

Hollow conduit: our body becomes a hollow conduit when we are letting go of the past and old energy. It is the time in our lives when we are waiting for something new to come about and give us clarity in our direction or decision-making.

Orbit: our orbit is where we give our attention. We often circulate or project our energy outward, but it is important that we give ourselves the energy to avoid cycling around maintaining everyone else's emotions.

Plandemic: the RKH term for the covid-19 "pandemic". I call it a "plandemic" because (to me) it was an orchestrated plan by the elite to create vulnerability.

Reincarnate: reincarnation in energy is like the "phoenix rising". This is the transformation inside your body and within your energy. Often, we feel "like death" when transforming, and it is because we are grieving our old selves.

Trilogy: the "people, places and things" that impact our life.

Some of the above mainstream words are not replacement for the generic definition, rather terms to help with explanation.